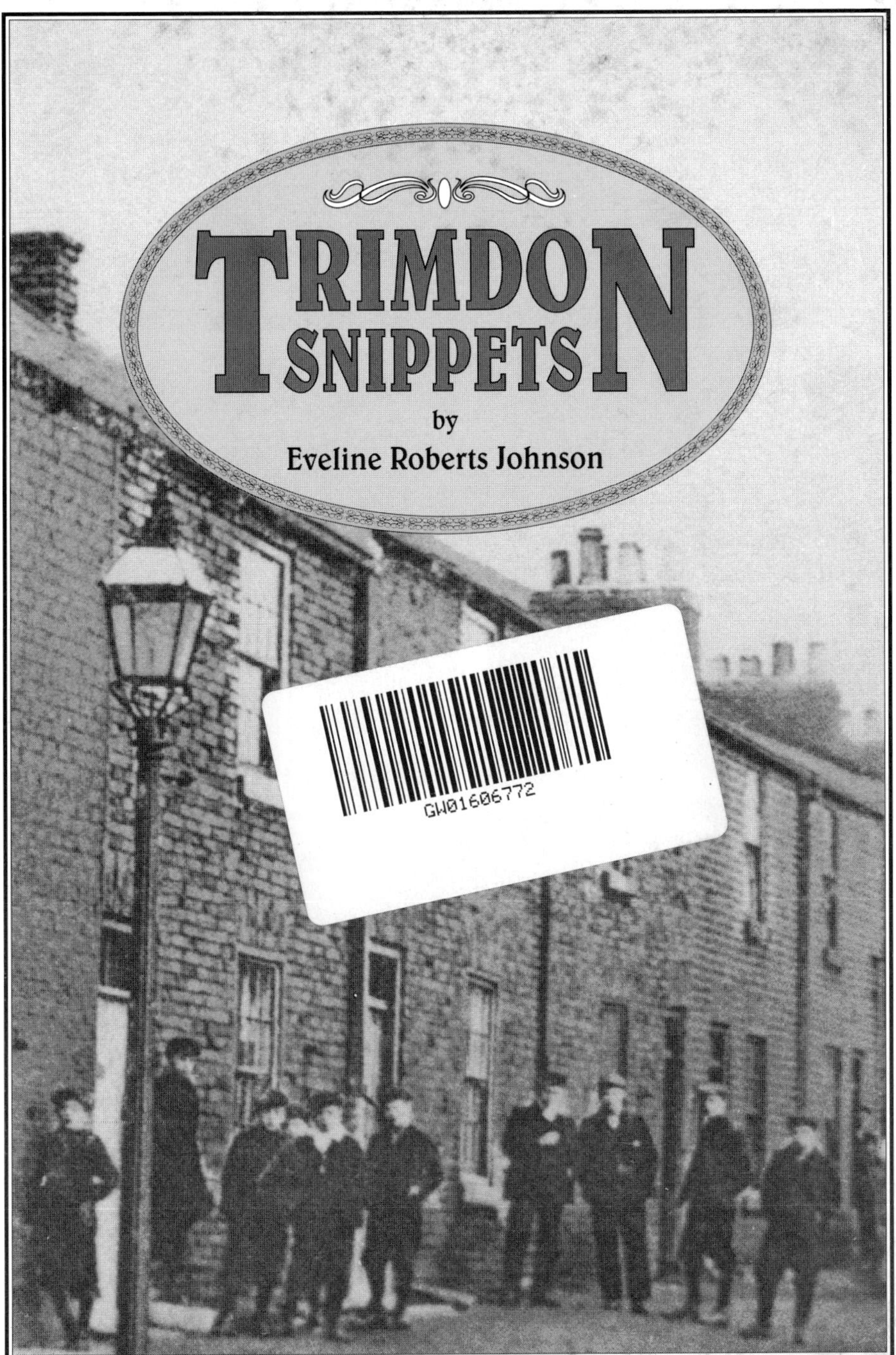
TRIMDON
SNIPPETS
by
Eveline Roberts Johnson
GW01606772

10 DOWNING STREET
LONDON SW1A 2AA

THE PRIME MINISTER

Eveline has worked and lived in the Trimdons for the past ninety years which makes her well qualified to write "Trimdon Snippets".

Her vivid recollections, her knowledge, her humour and her great love of the area make this a book that everyone will enjoy reading and will make them remember situations and stories that were part of their own past. Although her great interest is in local history, Eveline is still involved in the life of the area. Like me, she believes that while it is important to remember life in the three villages during the last century, we must also look forward to preparing the Trimdons for the new millennium.

Tony Blair

27 November 1998

Contents

Published by Printability Publishing Ltd.
with the assistance of Sedgefield Borough Council.
Thanks also to Easington District Council.

Printed by Atkinson Print,
10/11 Lower Church Street, Hartlepool TS24 &DJ.
Tel: 01429 267849 Fax: 01429 865416

ISBN No. 1 872239 26 9

Introduction

THIS is not a history of how the Trimdons came to be, but of the way of life at the beginning of this century. When I heard children asking the meaning of the words "pantry" and "fender" I realised how very different life is now.

Youngsters no longer seem to have an innocent childhood like those in the past. We no longer see them playing games in the street – games that taught them, without them knowing it, comradeship and the ability to share and also providing them with healthy exercise. Above all, parents knew where they were and so they could quickly be called home. When they wanted someone to begin a game they had a democratic way of deciding. Standing in a circle they would recite a rhyme like "Eenie, meanie, miny, mo, pointing to each one of the group separately until the chant was finished and the leader picked. It seems such a shame that modern children now have knowledge that only adults used to have. They were far more able to amuse themselves by inventing various games and never getting bored – games that cost nothing like imaginary shops and houses.

Men, especially miners, worked hard but so did the wives and mothers. It was non stop hard work but they did it knowing nothing of all the future labour saving inventions. Though at the time they were not considered important enough to warrant having a vote, they were the salt of the earth being able to care for and feed a family, often a very large family, on about 30 shillings a week (£1.50).

There is so much more we could have included in this book, but I hope that the reading of it might encourage more people to put their memories down onto paper. Some people call the past, the bad old days, but in many respects they were really the good old days. Times were more neighbourly and people lived without the fear of muggings and break-ins.

Thanks are due to all those who attended the late John Etherington's history class, and very special thanks to my colleagues Tony Magee for doing the typing and to Eddie Pike for printing the photographs from our Past and Present Exhibition.

I sincerely hope that this book will show the young ones what life used to be like and to revive some fond memories for the older ones.

Eveline Roberts Johnson.

Evolution of The Trimdons

ONCE upon a time, a long, long time ago, a wooden cross stood on top of a high hill. Later a church took the place of the cross with monks living beside it where the residential Tremenduna Home now stands. The little farming village surrounding the church became known as Trim and Dun meaning hill and water, because the river Skerne rises at Hurworth Burn where the white monks lived. Now the village is Trimdon and is parent to more villages bearing the name of Trimdon, which is very confusing to strangers who regularly lose their way.

Locals call the original settlement either Old Trimdon, or Trimdon Village but signposts just show Trimdon and leave the word village off, hence many visitors find themselves in the wrong village.

The Fox Covert

In the last century, prospectors started looking for coal, and with the financial help of the famous boxer, John Gully, a pit was sunk by the base of the Fox Covert, not far from Trimdon. A village grew around this pit and it was called New Trimdon, but later became known as Trimdon Colliery.

A few years later another pit was sunk from the other side of the Fox Covert, at Five Houses, which was by a stretch of water, the houses often referred to as being 'Over the Water'. As this was still in the Trimdon area, it was given the added name of Grange, after a very old farmhouse on the Watch Bank called 'The Grange; thus Trimdon Grange was born. As in the case of the first pit many houses were built for the miners and their families. They were built on what had once been a plantation of trees and that area is still known as the 'Planton' or to be precise the 'Plantation', even though all the houses are now modern ones.

The Grange, Trimdon Grange

A Plantation back street with netty. Grange pit heap towering over all.

Trimdon Station

With the growth of the railways, a passenger station was built behind Galbraith Terrace, but the station was later moved to the Trimdon Colliery area, so this area became known at Trimdon Station, yet the station part and the colliery are the same village. The main difference between the two parts is that the Colliery part belongs to Sedgefield Council and the Station part to Easington. Colliery people have soft water and Station folk have hard water.

For further confusion, another pit was sunk in the station area, and was given the name – Deaf Hill pit, so Trimdon Station itself is often referred to as Deaf Hill. No one seems to know how this pit got its name of Deaf Hill, but the nearest guess is that in days of long ago, if land was very poor, the old farmers would say it was 'deed' or 'dead' land, which perhaps has grown into the word deaf. The rising land behind the pit is called Sleepy Hill, which does not sound very productive.

More pit houses were built for the workers, to add to those that housed Foundry workers. This foundry had been moved to Spennymoor, but this now very modern part is still known as 'The Foundry'.

It is often said the name of Trimdon was given because King Canute on his barefoot walk to St. Cuthbert's shrine, at Durham, stopped here for a 'trim and wash down'.

THE DAY WE WENT TO TRIMDON

by Reg. Wright

The day we went to Trimdon,
It was wonderful, it was grand,
We heard the pit head buzzers blow,
We heard a big brass band,
We bought some tattie chips,
Oh what a lovely treat,
And ate them with our fingers in the street,
Out of Deaf Hill, thru the Foundry, past
the ancient Coffee Pot,
We found old Trimdon Village, like a
place that times forgot.

We sauntered down the Watchbank, where
a battle 'tis said was fought,
On Garmondsway, by King Canute, at least
that's what is thought,
We came to Trimdon Grange, people sometimes
just say the Grange,
And laughed at all the words that sounded strange,
There were netties, there were crackets, and
some other funny names,
And stotty cakes were made to eat, And not
for playing games.

They say the angels over there, have made
some pearly gates,
To set up in the Trimdons,
so the story tale relates,
And all the names of those who've gone
the legendary old
Will have their names emblazoned
all in gold
When the roll is called up yonder
we forever will recall
The day we went to Trimdon
was the greatest day of all.

THE BOLDEN BOOK

by Bob Dunn

As the North was not mentioned in The Doomsday Book of 1086, Hugh de Puiset compiled one in 1183. It is often called the Doomsday Book of the north and was the first survey of the north of the Tees - the area that was left out of the Doomsday Book. In the Bolden Book Garmondsway is mentioned as 5 bovates which belonged to Ralph Haget and which the bishop holds by his forfeiture and they yield 16s. 8d. and ten hens with one hundred eggs. And there the bishop has 4 bovates by his own purchase which lie waste.

In the Bolden book Trimdon is listed. The prior and Canons of Guisborough hold Trimdon in free, pure and perpetual alms, exempt from all payments and services for ever.

It is thought that the North was left out of the Doomsday Book because King William did not find Northern folk friendly.

CHOLERA IN SOUTH DURHAM

"The cholera has been very fatal in a colliery village named Trimdon, situated between the Ferryhill station of the York and Berwick railway and Hartlepool. It broke out very suddenly on Saturday fortnight and since then 14 deaths have taken place. Between 40 and 50 persons have been attacked with the disease in a bad form since its outbreak. Some of the deaths have been awfully sudden and without those premonitory symptoms that have previously marked the early stages of this terrible disease. The principal portion of the village is on a hill, and is rather favourably situated for sanitary arrangements, though there is a burning and sulphurous pit heap not far from that row. The disease has been most fatal among the least prudent, and hence poorer portion of the pitmen, though temperate regular living persons have fallen victim to it also. On Sunday evening week a Primitive Methodist local preacher, a pitman, conducted divine service in the chapel in that place and afterwards took a walk into the fields with his wife. He went to bed apparently in good health, about midnight he was attacked with cholera, in four hours he was dead. There was one death on Monday, and the medical men state the disease is quite epidemic. It is supposed to arise from some local cause not yet discovered, for, though surrounded by other large villages, no cases of cholera have been reported in them. Great complaints have been made with regard to the supposed negligence of the General Board of Health in London. Immediately upon the appearance of the epidemic in the village, Mr. Hood, the viewer and manager at the colliery, wrote to the proper authorities in London, informing them of the circumstances. Down to Saturday night no answer had been received by Mr. Wood. The cases have been attended to by Mr. Scott, the colliery surgeon, his assistant Mr. Gordon, and Mr. Haddock the union surgeon. The colliery surgeons instituted a house to house immediately upon the appearance of the disease".

The Square. Next to the Post Office was the Reading Room which had been the First Primitive Methodist Church.

LAND TAX

Land Tax was started as a means of gaining Government Revenue in 1759 and continued until 1830. Trimdon was no exception with two local collectors. The house itself was assessed including the amount of windows it had, the amount of servants it had, also any horses, carriages or carts. In the year 1783 Reverend Donnison of the village vicarage was obliged to pay tax on 29 windows. The least showing payment was 3 windows in 1793 land tax returns. So it may be assumed that anything less must have been free gratis. The Manor house was no exception, having to pay the pricely sum in the year 1760, the amount £4.14.0 in the name of Robert Roper Esq. A mere terrace house must have been as low as 8 pennies as some entries show. Such names as Mary Airey the charity benefactors, Woodifield, Beckworth, all paying large amounts, all having large estates somewhere in the old Trimdon. The total for 1760 to include all lands was £34.14.2.

Bryan Roper's house 1718.

A rigg is a cultivated strip in an open field shared by many people

..........*means a word is missed out.*

THIS INDENTURE MADE the twelfth day of June in the years of the reign of our Sovereign Lord James by the race of God King of England, Holland France and Ireland the thirteenth and of Scotland the nine and fortieth BETWEEN Humphrey Wharton of Gilling in the County of York gentleman and Thomas Wharton son and heir apparent of the said Humphrey on the one part and Brian Burleyson of Trimdon in the County of Durham yeoman on the other part WITNESSETH that the said Humphrey Wharton and Thomas Wharton for divers good causes and considerations them thereunto moving do by these presents devise grant and ....let unto the said Bryan Burleyson all that two houses and two cottages in Trimdon aforesaid now in the possession of the said Bryan Burleyson with all houses.......barns byres curtilage garths stackgarths (cow ?) yards gardens tofts crofts waterways easements passages profit and emolument whatever belonging to them. And also all that twenty acres of pasture ground be it mown or left lying and being in the East Field called the Coal pasture belonging to the cottagers of Trimdon. And also all those two riggs of which said riggs the one of them lying in the south croft of Trimdon aforesaid and the other rigg lieth in the north croft of Trimdon at the east end of Trimdon aforesaid and also all said acres of land lying and adjoining upon the west (nook?) of the said Brian

Burleysons garths in Trimdon called the (Wandases?) And also one parcel of ground adjoining upon the north end of the said five acres of land which parcel of ground aforesaid is a part or parcel of all the (Rye?) green with all and singular ways water passages easements profits and commodities whatsoever to the said land ground and premises belonging to or in any wise appertaining. All which said (premises?) are now in the tenure and occupation of the said Brian Burleyson or his assigns. Together also with full and free liberty for the said Brian Burleyson his executors administrators and assigns to water their beasts and bring them away presently from Martinmas until the first of May when and so often as need shall require at a certain place called (Dald.....?) and free egress and regress to and from the said watering place for a footway to the said watering place. And also way leave and liberty to fetch their water for their own use at the west well and little well lying on the north side of D...... the aforesaid so often as need shall require which said houses land ground and premises amongst other things the said Humphrey Wharton and Thomas Wharton have by grant and purchase to them and the heirs of the said Humphrey from the Right Honourable Phillip Lord Wharton and in Thomas Wharton heir apparent of the said Lord Wharton by deed of feofment indented the fourth day of December in the twelfth year of the reign of our sovereign Lord the King's Majesty that now is TO HAVE AND TO HOLD the said cottages ground riggs of land liberties and other the said premises above mentioned to be hereby granted with appurtenances unto the said Brian Burleyson his executors administrators and assigns from the feast of the Annunciation of the Blessed Virgin Mary last past before the date of these present unto the full end and term of nine hundred ninety and nine years thenceforth next ensuing fully to be complete and ended. YIELDING AND PAYING therefore unto the said Humphrey Wharton his heirs and assigns during the said term the yearly rent of thirteen shillings of lawful money of England at the feasts of Pentecost and St. Martin the Bishop in winter by even and equal portions or within fourteen days after being lawfully demanded. And doing....... and service during all the said term to the Court Leet and Court Baron of the manor of Trimdon aforesaid from time to time upon lawful notice and warning to be (given?) in that behalf. And if it happen that the said yearly rent of thirteen shillings or any part thereof or the said.... and service to the said Court Leet and Court Baron or either of them to be behind and not paid at any feast or time at which the same ought to be paid or done that then it shall and may be lawful for the said Humphrey Wharton his heirs and assigns into the said houses cottages or premises hereby demised or any part thereof to enter and distrain and a distress or distresses there found the same to take and drive or carry away and impound or withhold until such time as the said rent with all arrears thereof shall be duly satisfied and paid and until such times as the said Humphrey Wharton his heirs and assigns be sufficiently satisfied of and for his or their reasonable damage by and through not doing of the said..... and service AND the said Humphrey Wharton and Thomas Wharton the son and either of them do and duly by these presents for them and their heirs covenant promise and grant to and with the said Brian Burleyson his executors administrators and assigns that they the said Humphrey and Thomas his son or the one of them as or is at the time of the sealing of these presents lawfully seized of and upon the said houses cottages riggs of land ground and premises above mentioned to be hereby demised and of every part thereof with the appurtenances of .... a good pure perfect absolute and ......estate in fee simple in the law and have or hath full power and lawful authority to grant and demise the same with the liberty aforesaid unto the said Brian Burleyson his executors administrators and assigns according to the purpose tenor and effect of these presents. And that the said houses cottages riggs of land ground and premises now and so from henceforth during the said term shall be and continue to the said Brian Burleyson his executors administrators and assigns clearly and wholly acquitted compensated and discharged or otherwise...... the said houses cottages riggs of land ground and premises as the said Brian Burleyson his executors administrators and free assigns sufficiently saved and kept harmless of and from the manner of former bargains sales leases gifts entails grants contracts jointly .... titles of......titles of entry conditions condemnations judgements.....instructions signs for alienation and other such statutes.......... in the nature of statutes rent charges rent....arrears of rent and of and from all other manner of rights titles charges and encumbrances whatsoever heretofore had made done suffered ..... or occasioned by the Right Honourable Phillip Lord Wharton or Sir Thomas Wharton his son or by the said Humphrey or Thomas or any of them that it shall and may be lawful to and for the said Brian Burleyson his executors administrators and assigns from henceforth during the said term quietly and peaceably to have hold occupy possess and enjoy the said houses cottages riggs of land ground and premises with appurtenances without any lawful entry.... trouble eviction molestation hindrance or encumbrance had made or done by the aforesaid Phillip Lord Wharton Thomas his son or the said Humphrey or Thomas or any of them or any other by ...... or under them or..... preferments AND LASTLY the said Humphrey Wharton and Thomas Wharton his son and either of them do and say by these presents for them their heirs executors and administrators covenant promise and grant to and with the said Brian Burleyson his executors administrators and assigns that they the said Humphrey Wharton and Thomas Wharton his son their heirs and assigns shall and will at all and every time and times hereafter within the space of four years next ensuing after the date hereof make do acknowledge levy suffer and execute or cause to be made done levied suffered and executed all and every such...... and other act and act thing and things assurance and assurances in the law whatsoever either for the further or better assuring demising and granting of the said houses cottages riggs of land ground and premises with the appurtenances unto the said Brian Burleyson his executors administrators and assigns during all the said term of nine hundred and nine years for the granting and assuring the same with the reversion thereof to him the said Brian Burleyson his heirs and assigns or such other person or persons as he or his heirs shall appoint in fee simple to be charged with the said rent and .... as above is...... Be it by time or times with proclamation or without proclamation recovery or recoveries with double or single voucher or vouchers deed of feofment to be executed with .... of...deed or deeds enrolment... presented..... or confirmation with warranty against all as aforesaid or without warranty or by all or any one or more of the same ways or means or otherwise with warranty as foresaid or without warranty as by the said Brian Burleyson his heirs executors administrators or assigns shall be reasonably required at the cost and charges in the law of the said Brian Burleyson his heirs executors administrators or assigns for always that the said Humphrey Wharton and Thomas his son now and their heirs be not forced to travel for the doing thereof further than the city or county of Durham IN WITNESS thereof the parties aforesaid to these present indentures interchangeably have set to their hands and seals the day and year first above written.

Translated by Pam Fidiam and Valerie Portass.

This INDENTURE made the sixth day of October in ye eleventh year of the reign of our sovereign Lord William the third by the Grace of God of England Scotland France and Ireland King, defender of the faith etc. BETWEEN William Hickson of Little Town in the County of Durham, yeoman, and Alice his wife and John Hickson son and heir apparent of the said William of the one part and John White of Tursdale, miller, in the County afoesaid of the other part WITNESSETH that the said William Hickson and Alice his wife and John their son in consideration of the sum of five shillings of lawful money of England to them in hand paid by the said John White before the sealing and delivery of these presents the receipt whereof they do hereby acknowledge have demised granted and sold and by these presents do demise grant and sell unto the said John White ALL that his message or tenement and all those his several closes or parcels of ground situate and lying within the and territories of Fishburn hereafter mentioned, that is to say three closes of ground, one only called or known by the name of Park Flatts abutting and bounding upon the lands of Bryan Burleyson of Trimdon in the County of Durham, Gent., on the north And on the lands of Anthony Armstrong of Hart in the said County on the east west and south. And the other close commonly called the Newfall abutting and bounding on a close belonging to Gilbert Trotter called the Fall on the east and north and on the land belonging to the said Anthony Armstrong on the east and west and all that the barn or byre thereunto belonging together with all and singular houses edifices buildings barn byres stables orchards gardens battsides lands arable and not arable meadows feedings pastures common and common of pasture moorland heath woods underwoods trees and the soil and ground of the said woods underwoods trees hedges hedge roots mines and quarries of all sorts ways water watercourses paths passages profits commodities easements advantages emoluments hereditaments whatsoever with their and every of their appurtenances unto the said message land tenements hereditaments and premises above mentioned with them and every of their appurtenances or any of them respectively belonging or in any wise appertaining on to or with the same or any part or parcel thereof at any time heretofore had taken use occupied possessed or enjoyed or attested reputed or deemed taken or known to be as part and parcel or member thereof TO HAVE AND TO HOLD the message lands tenements hereditaments and premises above mentioned and every part and parcel thereof with their and every of their appurtenances unto the said John White his executors and assigns from the day next before the date of the date of these presents for and during the course of one whole year. Next including fully to be complete ended and run. To the intent and purpose only that by force and virtue of these presents of the statute for transferring uses into possession the said John White may be in the actual possession of the said lands and tenements of all and singular other the aforesaid premises and every part and parcel thereof with their and every of their rights members appurtenances enabled to take and attest of a grant release of the Re ??

Signed by William Alice and John Hickson but not by John White eleventh year of William the 3rd was 1698/99.

Mining and Work

JOBS

There was no picking and choosing of jobs when children left school at the age of 12, 13 or 14 when that was the age chosen by law. There were two main prospects – the coal mine for boys and service for girls. Service was literally what it said – to serve and work for others.

It must have been a very frightening experience for a young lad to be taken down the pit in the cage to work long hours in dark tunnels. A few boys might be lucky to be taken on in the shops. If it was the grocery business they had a lot to learn between running messages and delivering goods. As all tea, sugar, butter etc. came loose in crates or casks it all had to be weighed into pounds and packaged. It was quite an art to fold and tuck in a packet and if anything fell out you would have to start all over again. Butter had to be patted into pounds and half pounds whilst sides of ham had to be rolled and tied ready for cutting. Being a grocer was an exacting job but one in which they could take a pride.

Another lesson was the wrapping of goods. These packets were all neatly stacked onto brown paper and very properly wrapped and securely fastened with string. No-one could ever complain of a parcel bursting open. Tinned food was very rare mainly limited to salmon and pineapple. These were rare treats. Cakes and bread were never seen in the shops but in the towns there were often cream horns to be bought but nothing really fancy.

Sometimes a boy might be lucky to get a job in the colliery office as a helper at the station. If a boy wanted to be a butcher or a blacksmith they had to serve a very long apprenticeship. Of course, wages were just a shilling or two.

The Blacksmiths Shop, Deaf Hill Pit.

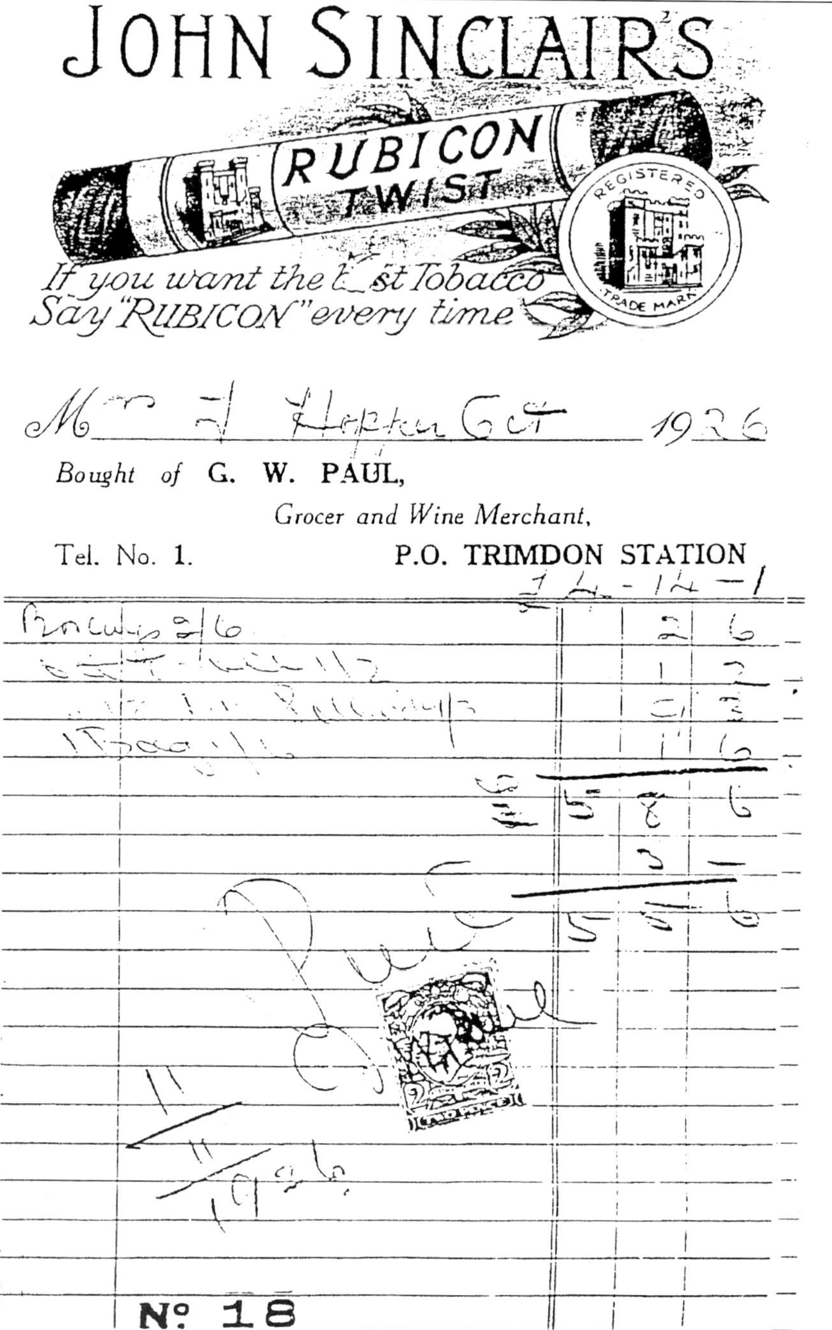

JOHN SINCLAIR'S

RUBICON TWIST

If you want the best Tobacco
Say "RUBICON" every time

REGISTERED TRADE MARK

Mrs ... Oct 1926

Bought of G. W. PAUL,

Grocer and Wine Merchant,

Tel. No. 1. P.O. TRIMDON STATION

Biscuits 2/6			2	6
			1	2
			[illegible]	[illegible]
			1	6
	£	5	8	6
			3	–
		5	5	6

№ 18

Youngsters who were not old enough for paid work were always on the look out for coppers, perhaps by shovelling coal into coal houses, minding horses or acting as a runner between the two picture houses.

Trimdon Motor Services (T.M.S.)

There was the Picturedrome at the Grange and the Imperial at the Colliery. The latter was built on the site of the first Wesleyan chapel and the former was near where the TMS garages were later built. They both belonged to the same people and they changed their programme every two days and on a Sunday. The show ran a serial (Tom Mix, Mary Pickford being favourites), a full length and news etc. While the Grange showed the first part of the show the Colliery showed the second part and they were then swapped over. To manage this they employed boys to run with the containers of film between the two halls. The boys really did run via the black path as this was before the first world war when there was no connecting road. Thus the owners could do two film shows for the price of one. The picture halls were not 'posh' places. They both had an upstairs and a downstairs. The front seats down below were wooden forms mostly for children - admission 1d. The halls did create a few jobs. There was the man who had to try to keep the children quiet, the person who took the money and the person who showed the films. To add to the enjoyment of the film there was a piano with a pianist who played music to match the picture. It was a puzzle wondering how to play soft music for the sad parts and then change to loud, quick time for the action parts-especially when the pianist was a blind lady. When films were shown at the Victory Assembly Rooms in George Street it was run by the family owners, The Markies. Madame Markie and her husband came from abroad and settled in Trimdon for a long while. The Picturedrome was once cleared very quickly when a teenager named Franklyn fell asleep and dreamed of a fire. When he woke up shouting 'fire', everybody thought it was for real.

There was also a nearby village attached to Trimdon. There was a pit, finished in the early 1900's and two rows of dwellings. The village was called Kelloe Winning. A little further along that road was the smallpox hospital. Though there were no patients by the second world war, people were still employed to keep it clean. It later became the site for a piggery. On that same road was Old Wingate Quarry (still in Trimdon), which is now called Wingate Grange Conservation area. This quarry, along with Garmondsway Quarry near Trimdon Village both employed men.

For an older person, a payment of half a crown - 2/6d. could be earned if he had a crake. Whenever a meeting or a sale was to be held he was employed to rattle his crake in the streets which made the residents come to their doors. He would then shout his news and so everyone knew what was going on.

If anyone managed to get employed by the Co-op they were over the moon because they were virtually assured a job for life.

A few girls would perhaps be lucky enough to get a job in a shop or maybe as a servant of one of the better off local families. But as mothers could not afford to keep girls at home unless one was very much needed the girls were obliged to move away. The surrounding towns people were always happy to hire a

Co-op Stores, manager Mr. Brown.

colliery girl, for they were known as good workers. When a girl obtained a situation, her few belongings were packed into a bass bag, a type of straw case, or packed into a brown paper parcel and then they were off to Hartlepool or Ferryhill for connections further away. Some girls were lucky to have a good mistress but some were not and there were no unions in those days. It was known for some employers to count the apples on the trees and to reckon up how many slices of bread could be cut from a loaf. Such people were so mean to think that a girl would steal extra food. The wage would be just a very few shillings per week most of which the girl would have to send home to the family. She would be lucky if she got one half Sunday off in a month. Other girls might be lucky and be with a decent, caring family and be well treated. The good mistress often gave cast off clothes to the girl for her family and extra food when she went home for her time off. In fact some mistresses and servants still kept in touch even after the girl had been married.

Some girls wished to do nursing. Here again there were vast differences. One hospital would not allow a nurse probationer to speak to a wardmaid. A nurse was never allowed to speak to a superior. She would never be allowed her proper time off and even her outside clothes would be criticised by the matron. For three months she received no pay but she would be given this money at the end of her three years in training. Once a month there would be a free half day. Patients had to stay in hospital much longer in those days. A simple appendectomy patient had to stay in bed at lest three weeks. Broken limbs had to be set and secured by wooden splints which meant that the patient was often bedfast. It was a great improvement when plaster casts came to be used.

Another hospital would have an entirely different attitude to its nurses. It would be much more friendly and honour the nurses off duty time. Nurses did work other than nursing, although it was part of their training. Wards were swept and dirty linen was cleansed before it was sent to the laundry. The ward kitchen had only a tiny fireplace and all of the breakfast eggs would have to be boiled on it. Breakfasts were served and cleared away but a maid did the washing up. The wage for a first year nurse was ten pounds a year paid monthly; in the second and third years it was £15 and £20 respectively. Uniform was black shoes, black wool stockings, dress with a three inch hem to the ankles, apron hem two inches above the dress, white starched collar to stud onto the dress, starched cuffs and a white cap. No married women were employed. Everyone slept on the premises and had to be in bed by 9.30 p.m. Board was given but it was not of good quality.

There were no unions to fight for workers rights. Nevertheless, even in these hard times, women at home often sang either favourite hymns or popular songs whilst working. Men and boys often whistled tunes as they worked or walked down the street.

PITS

The "old" pit as it was referred to, was sunk in 1839, mainly by the money of millionaire John Gully.

The Old Colliery.

Mrs. Bella Hill tells how her Grandfather Mr. Joseph Makepeace worked as a Sinker of this old pit. They used to descend in a bucket with one leg in the pail and one leg out to steer against the shaft. One day, a girder fell on his head and he had to go to see Dr. Russell. Fourteen stitches were put in the gash and then he returned to work ! ! When the cage was placed it came to ground level and the men walked straight in. One day a Mr. Lister and a pony went to go into the cage, but it was at the bottom of the shaft and so he and the pony fell down it and were killed. There was always steaming hot water from the boilers and the women living close by were able to take their buckets and collect red hot water on washing days. The engine to pull the trucks had a shape resembling a coffee

The way to the Foundry under the Station Bank.

pot, one of the reasons the nearby street was so named. The pit was closed in 1909. It left a dirty pit heap that stretched to Luke Street, but no one now could guess that, as it is all levelled and we have a good neighbourly Community Centre there.

The truck rails were first laid and crossed the road between Rodwell Street and Luke Street and went under the Archway that led to the Foundry houses. When it was found the engine was too tall to go through the Arch, the rails were re-directed straight to the station. The first shipment of coal to Hartlepool Docks was in 1843. By the pit yard were a few stone built cottages, this was called the Raff Yard. They only had one entrance at the back and the window touched the ground. They must have been very low for it was joked that a tall man could step outside from the bedroom window.

Coffee Pot Street.

TRIMDON GRANGE PIT

The Pit was sunk in 1845 by Joseph Smith, a Newcastle Merchant, and the place was called "Five Houses". It was presumed that there were only five houses there. They were very primitive and built of stone. Later, when more houses were built, the name was changed to Trimdon Grange. Trimdon being after the original Trimdon and Grange after Grange Farm which was nearby the Watch Bank where now stands "The Grange". By the Five Houses was a large pond, presumably to do with the pit, so when anyone wanted to go to Five Houses, they always called it, "Over the Water" (Ower the watter). One Thursday afternoon at 2.30 p.m., 280 feet down in the Harvey seam, there was a terrible explosion, this was on February 16th 1882 and many lives were lost. Much has been written about this horrible tragedy which left mothers without sons and wives with no husbands and no income to bring up a family. In 1847 further shafts were sunk and families came from Lancashire, Cornwall and Wales. Some Welsh people could speak only poor English.

Long Row and railway lines leading to Trimdon Grange Pit.

The population in :-

1801 was 278
1811 was 274
1821 was 302
1841 was 382 in 84 houses
1851 was 1,598 (836 male and 762 female adults in 324 houses).

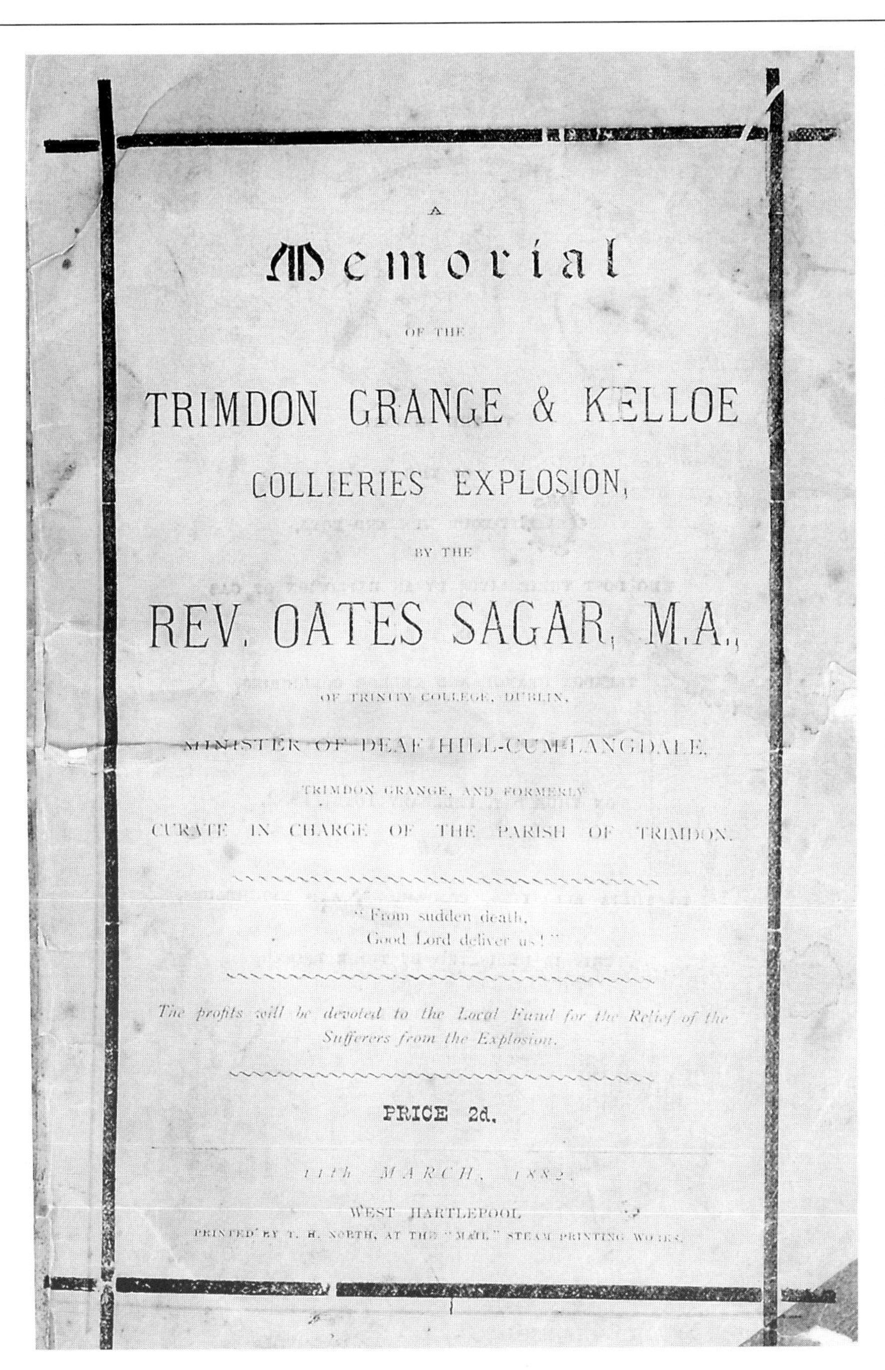

A

Memorial

OF THE

TRIMDON GRANGE & KELLOE

COLLIERIES EXPLOSION,

BY THE

REV. OATES SAGAR, M.A.,

OF TRINITY COLLEGE, DUBLIN,

MINISTER OF DEAF HILL-CUM-LANGDALE,

TRIMDON GRANGE, AND FORMERLY

CURATE IN CHARGE OF THE PARISH OF TRIMDON.

"From sudden death,
Good Lord deliver us!"

The profits will be devoted to the Local Fund for the Relief of the Sufferers from the Explosion.

PRICE 2d.

11th MARCH, 1882.

WEST HARTLEPOOL

PRINTED BY T. H. NORTH, AT THE "MAIL" STEAM PRINTING WORKS.

In 1852 the pit was sold to South Hetton Coal Co., but after 4 years sold to Walter Scott.

In 1881 there were 700 men and boys employed. Pits had names for their seams. Low main seam was 97 fathoms deep, Harvey 452 fathoms and Busty 149 fathoms. Some seams gave better coal than others. In 1863 Lady Londonderry owned the mineral rights. As the pit was failing from 1920 to 1925 it closed leaving 1,000 men and boys unemployed and then the 1926 strike made matters worse. It re-opened in 1937 when a rick 5 1/4 seam was found, but it was closed for good on February 16th 1968. The pit heap was one of the worst as it was almost on the Front Street, and seemed to hover over the Plantation Houses.

Fathom = 1.829 metres = 6 feet.

Mr. Arthur Davison wrote the following poem on the closure of Trimdon Grange Pit.

At last her long, long life is done,
Her troubles and her trials o'er,
Her head bowed now, her hope is gone,
She can give her best no more,
Her wheels are stilled, her chatter hushed,
This mother of a thousand souls,
But still her pride has not been crushed,
In man's demand for better coals,
A century and a half she's had,
And watched the village around her change,
Some for the good, some for the bad,
The grand old lady of Trimdon Grange.

Above her proud, majestic head,
She's watched the seasons come and go,
A shroud of mist, a sunset red,
A blanket white of flurrying snow,
In eighteen eighty two, there came,
Within her bowels, a mighty roar,
She carried on though just the same,
Remembering those who were no more,
Explosions, floods, all took their toll,
Right thro' her long tempestuous years,
Men paid the price to reap her coal,
But victory was always hers.

Mrs. Brown had lost a son,
Mrs. Jones her husband gone,
Who now will feed her growing brood ?
Clothe, and keep them all in food ?

At last her long, long life is done,
Her trials and her triumphs o'er,
She hasn't lost, she hasn't won,
She is gone and is no more,
Her memories will be bitter sweet,
To all who knew her in her day,
Until at last they fade and fleet,
And like her dust a blown away.

Where once she stood, the fields are green,
With beauty there on either hand,
Once more, a quiet country scene,
Once more a green and pleasant land.

PITMEN

Pitmen worked long hours below ground and for sustenance they would take a tin bottle of cold tea and some sandwiches in a tin bait-can. There was no means of washing hands down there, no rules of hygiene. This prompted a Trimdon Village man, Dennis Rowan to write this song:

"There's nee netties down the pit
so what's a chap to do".

This was set to music by Fishburn comedian Bert Draycott and then recorded by the first Trimdon Folk Group.

Of course smoking was not allowed below or there would have been explosions. Pit ponies were kept below ground housed in white washed stables and many friendships were formed between man and pony.

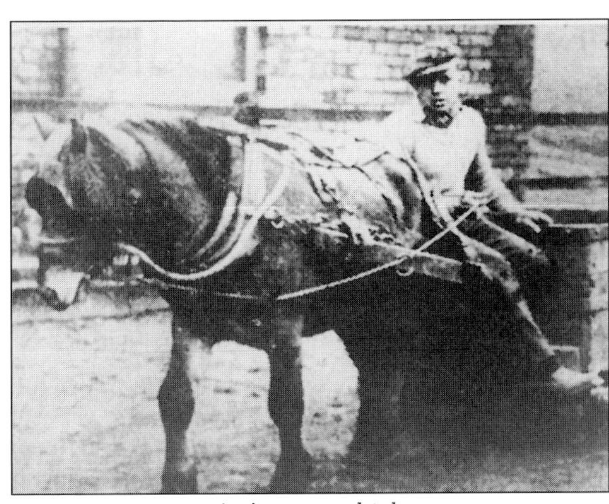

A pit pony and tub.

On May 22nd 1919, when Deaf Hill Pit was flooded, water rushed through like a tidal wave. A rescuer, Tom Hampson, found George Grey managing to cling to a roof prop surrounded by water up to his neck. Tom, a deputy overman, told the master shifter, who was a smaller man, to climb on to Tom's back and so they waded to safety.

THE TRIMDON GRANGE EXPLOSION SONG

Song written by Tommy Armstrong the Pitman's Poet.

Let us not think of tomorrow,
Lest we disappointed be
All our joys may turn to sorrow,
As we all may daily see.
Today we may be strong and healthy,
But how soon there comes a change,
As we may learn from the explosion,
That has been at Trimdon Grange.

Men and Boys left home that morning,
For to earn their daily bread.
Little thought before that evening.
That they'd be numbered with the dead.
Le us think of Mrs. Burnett,
Once had sons but now has none,
By the Trimdon Grange explosion,
Joseph, George and James are gone.

February left behind it
What will never be forgot.
Weeping widows, helpless children.
Maybe found in many a cot.
Homes that once were blest with comfort,
Guided by a Fathers care
Now are solemn and gloomy
Since the Father is not there.

Little children kind and loving
From their homes each day would run
For to meet their Father's coming,
As each hard days work was done.
Now they ask if Fathers left them
The Mother hangs her head.
With a weeping widows feelings
Tells the Child that Fathers dead.

God protect the lonely widow,
Help to raise each drooping head,
Be a Father to the Orphans,
Never let them cry for bread,
Death will pay us all a visit,
They have only gone before,
We may meet the Trimdon victims,
Where explosions are no more.

TRIMDON GRANGE AND KELLOE EXPLOSION 16.02.1882

List of those who lost their lives.

Buried in Croxdale, February 20th

Herman Carl Schier M.E. aged 23

Buried at Trimdon, February 19th

James Boyd	aged 13	Joseph Worman	aged 14
Joseph W.Burnett	aged 23	Thomas Worman	aged 13
George C. Burnett	aged 19	Patrick Durkin	aged 13
James Burnett	aged 17	Joseph Hyde	aged 23
William Burns	aged 35	William Jefferson	aged 18
Michael Docherty	aged 14	George Jefferson	aged 14
Edward Spencer	aged 19	John Williams	aged 31
William Jennings	aged 17	Michael McHale	aged 21
John Hale	aged 16	Thomas McHale	aged 13
Samuel Richardson	aged 17	George Simon	aged 16

Buried at Trimdon, February 21st

John Allison	aged 19	George Dobson	aged 26
Thomas Clark	aged 24	Thomas Peat	aged 21
Matthew Day	aged 13	Thomas Pryor	aged 26
John Smith	aged 26		

Buried at Kelloe, Sunday February 19th

Robert Edwards	aged 17	John Ramsey	aged 26
John Errington	aged 33	Frank Ramshaw	aged 17
Thomas Horden	aged 56	William Robinson	aged 34
William Madrell	aged 40	Ralph H. Robinson	aged 17
Christopher Prest	aged 45	George Slack	aged 21
Robert Soulsby	aged 60	Richard Thwaites	aged 27
Jacob Soulsby Jnr.	aged 27	John Wilson	aged 15

Buried at Kelloe, February 20th

Jacob Berriman	aged 33	John Hughes	aged 29
John Douglas	aged 13	William Parker	aged 16
David Edwards	aged 16	Thomas Sharp	aged 42

Buried at Kelloe, February 21st

Thomas Hunter	aged 37	Enoch Sayer	aged 18
William J. Hyde	aged 26	George Richardson	aged 29
Henry Joyce	aged 16		

Buried February 23rd

Peter Brown aged 60

Buried at Cassop-cum-Quarrington, February 19th

Thomas Blenkinsop aged 37

Buried at Shadforth, February 20th

Robert Maitland aged 40

Buried February 21st

Mathew French aged 13

The vicar of Deaf Hill-cum-Langdale was Rev. Oates Sagar M.A. who held a memorial service.

THE TRIMDON GRANGE EXPLOSION 16.02.1882

A POEM WRITTEN BY A YOUNG SURVIVOR

My story may be very old and very simple too,
yet, I know it to be truthful, and the truth is always new.
Oh yes, I know its simple, and very very plain,
but there's nothing half so beautiful as the old made new again.
God's goodness and his mercy are old, yet ever new,
his promises of grace and love, are faithful just and true.
And when I've told my story, I know you will agree,
that God has been kind and gentle, and merciful toward me.

I was brought up to attend the Sabbath school,
and very kindly taught to put my trust in Jesus who had my pardon thought,
and at a very early age, I gave my heart to him.
But soon, oh soon, I fell into wickedness, and sin.
Unmindful of my youthful vows, to live and spread his truth,
till face to face with death I stood, in the hopeful bloom of youth.
It was in a pit explosion at a place called Trimdon Grange/
When upward of a hundred men, were hurried to their graves.
Twas on the 16th day of February 1882.
Where I received such mercy, as I shall tell to you.

About half past two in the afternoon,
while my comrades around me sat.
We had just finished eating and were having a jovial chat,
when there was a sudden calm, and then a rush of air,
that put our lamps all in the dark to leave us in despair.
The cries were most heart rending of those who bent their knee,
and cried, oh God, be merciful, oh God, my God help me.

Two or three lay weeping while the others tried to pray,
"oh take me to my mother", was all the little ones could say.
We all with one accord got up, and stood in single file,
though it seemed a long way to the shaft, very nigh a mile,
When we took hold of each other, and got ready to march away.
I could draw that picture to my mind until this very day.

We hadn't travelled very far, when we heard someone behind,
it was a collier with a light, and oh, he was so kind.
As he came running to us, to take us by the hand,
Doing all that lay within his power, to help our little band.
We had not taken many strides, it seems so sad to tell.
We stumbled over a fall of stone, and put his light out as well.

It was so dark and dismal and what solemn thoughts struck me,
as I thought of my dear home and friends that I never more should see.
But bravely we struggled on, and helped each other too.
While the little ones so sadly cried, "Do take me to my mother now"
What had really happened, we could not truly tell,
Only as we came to the fire damp we all knew seriously too well.

For as we reached the after damp the collier to us should say,
"my lads, be very careful, here is someone lying on the way",
"It is the rolley wayman" one little fellow cried,
and all our little group save two, were lying by his side.
Bravely we struggled on, the collier and I,
while the rest of our companions had laid them down to die.
Manfully, we pushed along, as still onwards we crept,
We just got through the after damp, and then fell down and slept.
We may have slept three or four hours, it is difficult to say,
when a party of exploring men, to us had found their way.

They kindly shook and woke us up, by taking us to the shaft.
But we were so cold and trembling with lying in the draft.
And when they brought us up to bank, I was insensible.
Then, as I gradually came round, my joy I could not tell
to see my parents with me, and my brothers and sisters as well.
The joy and gladness in our home could be described to you.
Sadly I forgot God's mercies and the danger I had been in.
Rejected his offers of pardon, to keep living on, in sin.

But I do thank God now, I from my heart can say,
that my trust is placed in Jesus and my sins are washed away.
Now, whether my comrades have gone to heaven, is not for me to say.
Although they cried for mercy before they passed away,
Yet the thief upon the cross was saved at the eleventh hour.
And I hope to meet my companions upon your golden shore.
It may seem pleasant for a time to live in pleasurable sin,
but when death stares us in the face we stand in need of him.

Then let us all in Christ, united be, never let the world us sever.
So that in glory we may be for ever, and for ever.

Written by survivor George Robson

He grew up and became Alderman George Robson.

Miners ready for underground.

LOCAL MINING TERMS

Afterdamp

Carbon Dioxide - a lethal gas an aftermath of an underground explosion

Back Canch

Roadway enlargement away from the working face.

Back Shift

Afternoon shift e.g. 2.00 p.m. - 10.00 p.m.

Bank

Surface area of the Colliery

Banksman

Person in charge of winding operations involving the cage at the surface and linking with the underground (shaft bottom onsetter) and the winding engine man.

Brass

Iron pyrites - similar to pieces of metal brass within some seams of coal

Canch

Stone (rock) above and below the coal seam removed to form a roadway.

Cavils

A draw (lottery) to determine without prejudice who works where at production level.

Check Weighman

Mineworker representative (union official) whose initial duty was to check the weight of the coal within tubs on behalf of the miner.

Chock

A roof support usually at the edge of the roadway made up of a number of blocks of solid wood.

Cross Cut

A minor roadway linking two major roadways.

Cut

The area of the coal face where the coal has been removed by a coal cutting machine prior to shot firing then further removal of the coal.

Datal Worker

Miner on standard wage earnings without any additional bonus or piece-work payments.

Deputy

A Supervisor who is deputy to the Overman with specific statutory duties involving safety inspections and gas monitoring. He also has First Aid qualifications.

Downcast Shaft

The mine shaft from the surface to an underground level down which the air is drawn into the mine for ventilation.

Endless Rope

A haulage system to which both empty and full tubs are attached and can be hauled in both directions. (Inbye and outbye).

Filler

A coal face worker as part of a team who shovels prepared and loose coal from the working face to an adjacent conveyor belt.

Firedamp

A combustible hydro-carbon gas-methane which if allowed to accumulate due to inadequate ventilation can be the cause of an explosion if ignited.

Fore Overman

The senior official in charge of an underground district.

Goaf / Waste

The vacant area left behind as the coal advances after supports have been removed.

Headgear

The surface structure and equipment at the head of a mine shaft.

Heading

A roadway usually driven separate from the coal face.

Overcast

Air crossing a sealed roadway crossing another roadway as part of the ventilation system.

Overman

An underground official in charge of underground operations on a shift basis. e.g.

Fore Overman - Senior official responsible to the colliery Undermanager.
Fore shift Overman - early shift overman
Back shift Overman - day/afternoon shift overman
Master Shifter- night shift (tub loading) overman.

Plough

Coal face production machine designed to rip coal from the face as it is hauled in each direction, the coal is automatically deposited onto a chain conveyor.

Putter

A worker who moves tubs manually.

Ripping

Removing stone (canch) usually above the extracted seam to form a or enlarge a roadway.

Stonedust

Crushed / powered limestone spread throughout the mine to render coal dust accumulations on outbye roadways incombustible.

Sump

An area below normal level where water is allowed to drain to facilitate pumping operations.

Tub

A four wheeled container used for the transporting of minerals and materials.

Tailgate

Roadway at the opposite end of a longwall face to the maingate or mothergate, normally return airway from the working face and access to it for materials including roof supports.

Kerf

The gap left in the coal face after the operation of the coal cutting machine.

Kervings

Coal cuttings produced by the operation of the coal cutting machine.

Kist

Deputies district operational base (desk).

Landing

A wider than normal section of the roadway designed to accept a number of both empty tubs for loading and loaded tubs for transport out bye to the shaft bottom landing.

Loading Point

The terminal point of the conveyor system where the mined coal on the conveyor is transferred into empty tubs at the landing.

Longwall Face

A method of mining where a length of coal face, 200 metres in length is extracted and moved forward with a roadway at each end of the face driven at right angles, named maingate or mothergate and tailgate.

Main and Tail

A rope haulage system where the main rope at one end of a train (set) of tubs hauls in one direction and the tail rope hauls in the opposite direction.

Onsetter

The worker who is responsible for the cage loading and unloading at the shaft bottom with signalling links with the surface Banksman.

Outbye / Inbye

Outbye is the underground area of the mine approaching the shaft bottom and Inbye is the area of the mine approaching the production area.

Upcast shaft

The mine shaft from an underground level to the surface where a powerful air extraction unit draws air from the surface, through the downcast shaft throughout underground workings and completes the ventilation system.

Wind

Compressed air for use of pneumatic equipment.

Windy Piele

Compressed air driven pneumatic drilling machine

Terms given by Tom Watts.

TRIMDON GRANGE TRAGEDY

It happened on November 19th 1926, the year of the National Miners strike.

During Industrial Depressions, it was the practise of miners, at least in Durham County, to dig for discarded coal in the pit heaps.

At Trimdon Grange, two local men entered an abandoned cavern to obtain coal when the sides caved in, partially burying Herbert Owens, aged 21, of Oswald Row. His perilous position was soon realised but while other men were tunnelling to extricate him a further collapse of the sides took place, completely burying the man.

The would be rescuers increased their efforts to release Owens, and three times rope was passed under his shoulders and three times attempts were made to pull him out.

The unfortunate man however, was wedged in, and the sides continued to fall. Shoring the sides with timber was resorted to. At 5.00 p.m. it was decided to make a new tunnel into the heap to endeavour to release him, and shifts of six men wearing gas helmets, worked frantically but it was 10.00 p.m. before Owens was got out, his body was in a very bad condition being almost burned by the nature of the heap.

Playing leading roles were two local men, Mr. John Beattie and Mr. Joseph Clark, who with total disregard of their lives, faced extreme danger. They were both awarded the George Cross for their brave efforts.

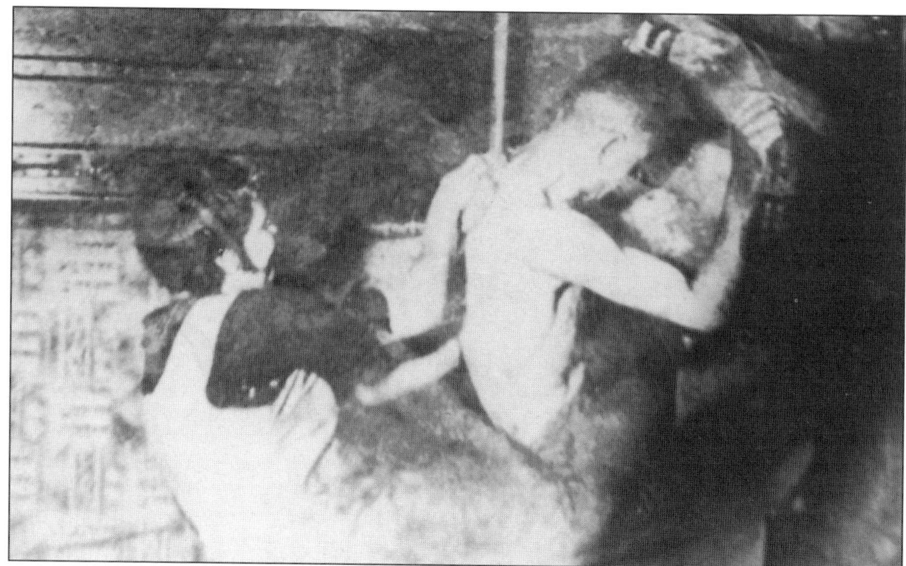

A pitmans bath time.

TRIMDON GRANGE PIT HEAP

by Tony Magee

I'm sure that someone can tell me that I'm wrong but I just can't think of any other mining village whose pit heap dominated the village the way Trimdon Grange's did. It stretched from the back road leading from Trimdon Village to the Whinney Moors on the Kelloe road (the Back Ower Lorrin as we called it, although I have never seen this written down before and so I can't vouch for the spelling - or the accuracy of the phonetics for that matter) right down to the front street of Trimdon Grange and it skirted the Western Edge of this road from St. Alban's Church almost to the right hand turn into the new road down to Trimdon Colliery. It was immense and its enormity was reinforced by the perhaps 80 degree angle of the slope as it rose to its summit of perhaps 150 feet. First time visitors to Trimdon must have been stunned by its dark bulk looming over the village, but to us its presence, though felt in several ways, usually went unnoticed. Generally speaking it was just there; though it was noticeable that in summer any part of the village which fell in its shadow - and that was the vast majority of it - tended to get an hour or two less direct sunlight than did the rest of the area. However, as if by way of compensation, in winter, when the snow came, Trimdon Grange was blessed with its own private Tyrol and, if in summer the pit heap looked drab and dirty, it was transformed spectacularly by the winter snow.

Trimdon Grange Pit.

If you had traversed the pit heap from the Back ower Lorrin to the front edge facing the village you would have seen two completely different aspects. At the beginning of the walk the heap was not nearly so high as the front side and was uniformly grey with no sign of vegetation. On reaching the plateau, the desolation stretched before you as far as you could see and there was no sign that there might be any type of community in the vicinity. The walk across the top of the heap was what I would imagine a moonscape to be, dark barren and dangerous. Occasionally you would have to jump or clamber across dried up beds of rivulets spontaneously formed during the last wet spell. I personally would not have attempted such a walk if the weather had been wet enough to be still feeding these streams. On the approach to the front edge of the heap, plants began to appear till you reached the crest of the front edge to see Trimdon Grange lying below. Beneath your feet, stretching to the road below, the heap plummeted in a cascade of vegetation, grass at first to be joined by a swathe of ferns then brambles, trees and shrubs at the foot of the slope. Although it wasn't the hanging gardens of Babylon by any means, the front of the heap did, at least, present a pleasant aspect to the village from this side. To descend you had to go down in two stages, a third of the way then a relatively flat area about twenty yards across followed by the final plunge down to the road along one of several well worn pathways. On the side of the heap nearest the pit an area had been flattened and enclosed to form the stocking ground. This was connected to the pit by an aerial walkway and to the main road below by a winding dirt track emerging near the signal box, which was on the opposite side of the road to the private house just down from the Dovecote.

Trimdon Grange Colliery Banner.

Of course, the pit heap was out of bounds to us children – which meant, inevitably, that we frequented it far more than we would have done had we been actively encouraged to play there. It was a wilderness in which we could fight our wars, in which we could explore and which we could use as a resource in our chasing and hiding games. But more than this, it was an adventure playground and it was private. It was one of those places - every town and village has them - where adults just did not go, or at least if they did we rarely saw them and they probably would have preferred that we did not see them as any adult who wanted to be up there was probably up to no good. On the heap we could light fires, shoot air rifles, slide down on the scree on rubber belting discarded from the pit and risk our lives in numerous ways which were just fun then, but which now, with the benefit of hindsight, quite frankly appall me.

I think that the pit heap ceased to be fun to me in my early teens. I remember quite clearly walking past the school which is now The Community Centre on a very wet and grey day. The rain had been torrential and the road at that point had been almost totally covered with water that had run off the heap. Little sandbanks, or perhaps slagbanks would be a more accurate description, were forming on the road due to the action of the water. I remember thinking what if the water was washing down more material than the few inches that was gathering on the road in front of me. How much does it need to wash down before the whole lot comes sliding down after it? At the time it was only a year or two after Aberfan where 144 people including 116 children had been killed when a pit heap had slipped down onto that village and engulfed the local school and I suddenly became worried that it could happen here too. All the years the heap had been standing there and if it ever slipped there was a school directly in its path along with shops and hoses on the main road. Maybe I was just becoming too old to be frolicking about on the pit heap the way I had done as a child, but whatever the reason I would never see it in the same way again. And, in a way, that was just as well. In a few years it would be gone along with the pit buildings, the railway, the signal box, the plantation, the front street, and the majority of the facilities in the recreation ground. Trimdon Grange was changing and so was I. Maybe that's why I retain such a fondness for the place; you often do for old friends you grow up with.

Tony Magee
21 / 2 / 96.

DEAF HILL PIT

This pit was sunk in 1870 and closed for good on 24th February 1967. No one can really find out the origin of the word Deaf Hill. The nearest solution I think is when land did not yield much, it was called "deef" or dead (deed) land. The name of the ecclesiastical parish is Deaf Hill cum Langdale (Langan Dune) which means the long valley, and there is a long valley behind where the pit was, and the hill by the footpath to Wheatley Hill was called Sleepy Hill, which might refer to the old timers idea of deaf or dead land. The first Vicar, Dr. Sagar of St. Paul's lived in the vicarage at the top of Sleep Hill looking over the quarry. This was later the Coal Board Farm

In 1919 the pit was flooded and a pony drowned. It was through the hard work of the Officials and volunteers that it got into production again. The pit was idle for 6 months.

Deaf Hill Pit, pre-War.
Shows pit heap and timber stacked in yard; 3 houses in pit yard.

Temperance Band at Durham Gala 1924.
Banner draped in black for a fatal accident during the year.

In 1944 Hutton seam was closed and 160 men went to Blackhall Colliery via T.M.S. buses

In 1951 Deaf Hill was awarded production bannerette for the greatest proportionate output in County Durham during the last year.

In 1955 surface work combined with Wingate Colliery, when the plant for dealing with coal at Deaf Hill was dismantled, and a light railway was laid for Deaf Hill coal to be drawn overland to Wingate.

In 1956 Junior Ambulance team won National Competition.

Deaf Hill Pit closed on 24th February 1967.

97 men went to Easington Pit
70 men went to Blackhall Pit
45 men went to Thornley Pit
49 men went to Shotton Pit
76 men made redundant by age or illness
61 men retained for salvage
5 men moved away to Warwickshire
12 men moved to Mansfield.

Deaf Hill Rescue Brigade.

In 1910 a Rescue and Aid was passed so a few men from Deaf Hill pit travelled by pony and trap to Houghton - le - Spring for instructions. They learnt the use of breathing apparatus, gas testing with canaries and first aid. Later they had more equipment. In those early days when a man was lamed (injured) he was either carried home on his mates back or , if the injury was severe, he'd be transported in the horse wagon. Men were paid fortnightly on a Friday. The week when they had no pay was called Baff week, so insurances, bills etc., were all collected on pay week. Three marrers (mates) worked in different shifts, fore, back and night. One marra who was not at work would collect their pay slips from the Colliery office and then collect the pay according to the amount of work done.

Many houses had a slate on their wall with a time chalked on it. This was for those in first (getting up to go to work very early in the morning). This was a guide to the "Caller up" man.

He came round to knock up the men to make sure they would get to work. Very useful for those without an alarm clock. He often used a long stick to tap on the bedroom window.

There were good places, bad places, and worst places for working down the mine, some narrow, small or wet. To attempt fairness these places were drawn for, four times a year, and they were called the Cavils. The women on that day did various superstitious things to ensure a good cavil (place) for their men. The workers in the pit had very close relationships and were always ready to help each other.

COKE OVENS

Near to the Grange Pit and opposite where the T.M.S. Garage was built were the Coke Ovens, believed to have originally been built by a German firm. That is why during the first World War people were afraid the zeppelins would attempt to drop their bombs on the site. However, the nearest place to receive a bomb in the first war was at the Knicker Bocker Lane by Town Kelloe.

Across the way was a reservoir which, sad to say, was the cause of a few drownings. It was created by the water being pumped from the pit. The ovens were closed down for a few years, relit in the 40 - 50's but finally closed in the early 60's. In its last phase, an aerial flight was erected for Transport over to the reservoir which is now no more. The ovens produced gas and petrol. According to Mr. George Dawson, the gas was sent to Hartlepool in a pipe line parallel to the railway. Trimdon people did not have any, they just had their fires alight by the Colliery free coal. During the Second World War two airmen had to bale out by parachute, and thought they were in for a dunking when they saw the reservoir water, however they came safely down on land.

The Coke Ovens, Trimdon Grange.

DEAF HILL COLLIERY 1958

Deaf Hill Colliery was sunk by the Trimdon Coal Company in 1870, and from 1900 until the present day, from information supplied by Mr. John Hampson (Rolleywayman), 75 years of age, whose name is perpetuated with a haulage curve known as "Hampsons Curve", there have been 11 Managers.

In 1919 the Colliery was idle for 6 months, following the break in of heavy feeders of water from the Harvey Seam workings approaching the Butterknowle fault at the southern extremity of the take. The Colliery was partially flooded until satisfactory dams were built in the Hurworth District of the Harvey Seams.

In 1921, the Trimdon Coal Company was taken over by the South Durham and Cargo Fleet concerns, and came under the management of Messrs. J. H. B .Foster, and Geo. Raw, both well known Durham Mining Engineers.

Peak output was reached in 1939, when 363,356 tons were produced. From 1939 until 1945 output declined, due to the exhaustion of the good Low Main and Harvey seams. Since 1945 production has been maintained between 160 and 170 thousand tons per annum. In 1955 the figure was raised to 186 thousand tons and in 1956, 223 thousand tons were produced.

In September 1955, the Wingate and Deaf Hill reconstitution scheme was partly completed and put into operation. It briefly consisted of scrapping the 10cwt. tubs in favour of one ton tubs, and transporting them from Deaf Hill to Wingate via the overland narrow gauge railway by means of 75 h.p. diesel locomotives where the coal was tipped at the new tipper station, which transported the coal from both Wingate and Deaf Hill to the Wingate washer.

The colliery, at the present moment, is producing 5,500 tons per week from the Hutton (section 2′ 3″) and the Busty Tilley (section 3′ 9″) seams, both containing two dirt bands.

Power loading by the Flighting methods is working well in the Hutton seam and it is visualised that eventually the colliery will be loading all its coal at the present loading point, 300 yards from the shaft bottom. This will further improve the colliery's figures.

The Colliery Junior Ambulance Team won the Area competition in 1954, the Area and Divisional competition in 1955 and the Area, Divisional and National competitions in 1956, they were unsuccessful at Blackpool in the 1955 National Competition. Mr. Fred Hope, the Ambulance Attendant for the Colliery, was awarded the B.E.M. in 1955.

In 1952 the colliery was awarded the Output Banner by the Durham Branch of the National Union of Mineworkers.

In 1957 the colliery will be an all electric colliery, steam winders being replaced by electric powered winders – this will be the completion of the re-organisation.

This article was by a writer unknown
Submitted by Muriel Spresser

BANNERS

Every pit liked to have its own banner. These were very much revered, and were brought out on special occasions. The highlight of course, when it was paraded, accompanied by a brass band at the Durham Miners Gala, held once a year in Durham City. This was said when the Miners went ' to get their rights'. The day was looked forward to , by old folk, young folk, and babes in arms, met up with friends and relations from different parts of the country, shopkeepers barricaded their windows in case of accidents. In each village early morning saw the band collecting and if there was no local one, then an outsider would be hired.

The pitmen had drawn lots for the honour - and - pay - of carrying the banner. This was not always an easy task, as well as the two poles, there were cords to be held, and if it was a windy day it became very difficult.

Apart from the actual carcuas or silk banner, there were many other parts, a crossbar where the top of the banner was attached, with a long pole at each end of the crossbar. Thick cords hung down for bearers to hold, to steady the banner, and the pole bearers were fitted with leather harness ending in cups for resting the end of the poles whilst the banner was being carried.

Silk and gold was prominent, gold silk fringes, gold wool cords for holding whilst the banner was being carried.

If a fatal accident had happened during the year, the top of the banner was draped in black. An artist, using gold paint for decoration would paint particulars of the lodge owning the banner with a scene, sometimes religious on one side, and popular leader's photos or scenes on the reverse.

Popular makers of banners were Tutill of London and Bainbridge of Newcastle.

DEAF HILL BANNERS

In 1892, Deaf Hill had a banner made of canvas by Bainbridge of Newcastle. It had a religious scene on one side and three men on the other side. They were Mr. Peter Lee (who was born in Trimdon Grange), Mr. Hughes (who was the first Labour M.P. for Chester - le - Street) and Mr. Teddy O'Neil (who lived in 19 Rodwell Street and at 2 Railway Street, Trimdon Station).

After a time, the Banner grew worse for wear, and the edges grew ragged, so it was decided to have a new one. But what was to be done about the shabby one ?

Eventually it was decided to have a grand raffle for the pit employees and the prize would be the 1892 banner.

The winner was a Mr. Darby - his first name was not known - Of course it was too big to get into a Colliery house, so the shabby surround was cut off leaving the picture.

1st Deaf Hill Banner.

It was presented to Mr. O'Neill and his wife, and it has passed down through the O'Neill family, the present owner now being Mr. Ted Atherton, who works in Saudi Arabia.

The little scene on the banner seemed to have illustrated 'The Good Samaritan' with the traveller's white horse standing by. We do not know the actual date of the new, second banner, but from a photograph it was in existence (plus black drapes) in 1924 when it also showed "The Good Samaritan" but this time with a black horse. There is no picture we know of which shows the other side.

The present banner hanging in the Community Centre (Welfare Hall) has the Samaritan with a Black Horse still, and the reverse side shows Conishead Priory.

It is questionable if this is a second or third banner, because I heard once that the banner had been severely damaged in a drunken brawl and so had to be replaced.

Deaf Hill Banners.

TRIMDON GRANGE BANNER

A new banner from Trimdon Grange was purchased from Tutill of London in the summer of 1929, so it sounds as if this one replaced an earlier one. The decoration was a Biblical one with the words "Unity is Strength". The reverse side shows a picture of four men shaking hands in unity. They represented England, Scotland Ireland and Wales, the Scotsman wearing his kilt. It is not known what happened to this one, but a new banner was unfurled on Friday July 19th 1963.

The ceremony was performed by Mr. Harold Wilson who said he was delighted with the spirit of comradeship in the village. He had a delightful time. This banner now hangs in the Grange Community Hall. Sadly part of the base caught and was torn on some bushes when it was paraded at the dedication of the pit wheel. An enthusiast, Mr. David Gibson had it repaired, and also ran a successful campaign to fund the cost of a new banner.

Sometimes unused Banners were sold to other Lodges when they had their own decorations painted over the old.

When a miners lodge meeting had to be held, the men were notified by the crakeman. He would travel all the streets of the village shouting "Meeting at 7 o'clock, tonight in Miners Hall". There was no excuse then for anyone not knowing.

The old pit. (John Gully)

Leisure & Railways

ADULT INTERESTS

Football, of course, was the tops with Cricket a close second. The main playing ground at Trimdon Station was on the moors, behind Station Road. A beck ran through the centre - the footballers using the right side, the cricketers using the left, where they had an old railway coach as a pavilion. This was where the wives made the tea for the visiting teams. At Trimdon Grange there was even a women's football team.

Deaf Hill Juniors AFC 1906-7.

Quoits was a competitive game. It was an iron ring which was thrown on an iron stake in the ground; the object being to completely encircle the stake. There were teams travelling and competing for points in the various villages.

Handball was another competitive game played against a very high wall which was sometimes purpose built. Handball or "Fives" was a skilled game played at what was called the ball alley at the Workman's Club. The idea was to 'stot' the ball and see it rise against the wall. Competitions were arranged with visiting village teams. The first game played there was won by Demsey Gorton against Joe Elliot of Trimdon Grange. The game must have been popular many years ago as it is known that a man named 'Pompey' was champion of England.

Whippet racing and pot share bowling were also competitive pastimes.

Deaf Hill Cricket Club – pre-1914-18 War.
Matches were played on the moors.

Apart from the pubs there were also reading rooms in the villages. The Colliery room was the building that had once been the Primitive Chapel in the square.

Many men kept pigeons and raced them, housing them in the Crees they built which were called pigeon lofts. The trains were used to carry the baskets of pigeons to the starting points of their races.

The women, poor souls, had no such pastimes. They were not even able to visit the pubs. The few people who liked their beer would send a child with a can or a jug to the side door of a pub to buy their refreshment.

They gained their outings or meetings if they were members of the church Mother's Union or the Chapel's sisterhood. When funds were needed these members would meet sometimes in each others homes and sew for chapel or church sales of work. Pillowcases, petticoats, aprons etc. would be made, and many people saved a few pence weekly which would be paid out at the time so that they would have money to spend at the sale.

Life for some was much improved when Miss Florence Purvis proposed to start a Womens institute. Originally the scheme was to help women and the war effort throughout various countries. It was a place where demonstrations and talks were given as well as entertainment. The meetings were held once a month at Trimdon Grange; later one was started at Trimdon Village when the Community Hall was built. For making tea and washing up in the Temperance Hall, water had to be carried from a house in the Foundry. Later the meetings were held in the Welfare Hall and later still in the Community Hall in Wingate Road. This hall was originally built during the war as a nursery so that mothers could work in factories for the war effort. The present Trimdon Grange Clinic was, likewise, a nursery.

Women's Fellowship Tea for old folk in Church Institute.

For teenage girls there was the Girls Friendly Society run by Mrs. Whitehead, wife of the vicar of St. Paul's Church, Trimdon Station. They were encouraged in all skills such as drama, singing, needlework, country dancing. Competitions were held and the winning club or individual of the diocese would go to the Albert Hall for the all England competition. Gladys Nattress won her way there and won a first for Deaf Hill, St. Paul's.

There was also a group of Girl Guides belonging to that Church, but it was not confined to the Church Members only.

GAMES

Children's games were often governed by the seasons. It was funny how no-one told the children when to start playing different games, but they seemed to emerge automatically. For instance, Spring time and Easter brought out skipping ropes. Not expensive ones with lovely handles, but a length of rope cut from the old clothes line. Individual skippers would have competitions, such as seeing how fast they could go, doing and singing 'Pitch patch pepper' then reciting the alphabet. Another one was skipping with arms crossed and using the rope backwards. Other fancy tricks were also used.

A group of children played together, a child holding each end of the rope, and turning it while the rest took turns to follow and skip.

A favourite was to skip whilst saying "Tell me the name of your young man", then skip ever so quickly to the turning of the rope while reciting the alphabet. When they made a mistake in the skip, the letter they stopped on would be the initial of the young man.

Rose Street (Chapel Row) showing gas street lamps, Trimdon Grange.

These ropes were also used for jumping over, the rope getting higher and higher.

There were no playing fields but games were played at the front of the houses or in the back streets which were just ways, not made up at all. Another interesting game of skill was 'Itchy Dabber'. Large squares were marked out and numbered, then with an old empty shoe polish tin, turns were taken to get the tin into the bays the least number of times, pushing the tin with the side of the foot, whilst hopping on one leg.

Tops and whips were for both boys and girls, seeing who could keep it spinning the longest. The top of the whips had coloured chalk marks on them which made a galaxy of colour when in motion.

Diabolo was another game, two thin sticks joined by a length of string with a thick round piece of wood with a narrow waist in the middle, which was thrown in various different ways from the middle of the string.

Chucks could be bought but were often just cube like pieces of wood or such. These were played on the back of the hand and the skill was to see how many could be used at once.

Another back of the hand game was buttony. A bay (square) was marked on the ground containing a few buttons or perhaps a special one. The person who twitched a button from her hand to cover a button in the bay was the winner of that button.

Little girls collected 'boodies' - bits of broken china or stones, and these were used as shop articles with small pieces of grit as money. These 'shops' were often played on the netty steps. At least the kiddies all played near their homes and the mother just had to shout the child's name when he or she was wanted.

The boys played marbles in the back street, it was easy to scoop a hole for the marbles. Penkers and marbles were much prized and carried in trouser pockets.

A boy was thrilled if he had a metal booler, if not metal, anything round, like the later hula hoop. The metal ones often came from the blacksmith's shop at the pit, all with a metal rod with a curved end. This was used to set and keep the booler moving, the boy running with it, enabling a lot of ground to be covered.

Block was an all round game. One picked to hide while the rest closed eyes and counted to 50 or more, then shouting 'off' they singly set off to find the hide out. The winner then taking the role of hiding.

Mounty kitty was not an easy game for it was jumping on each others backs.

Flicking over collections of cigarette cards to try and win more was another pastime.

Naughty ones in that time played 'Nocky Nine Doors'. One child would knock on someone's door and they all ran to hide, and watch the householder looking round for their visitors.

Indoors on winter nights, they could play quiet games, or a bit noisier ones like 'Snap', 'Snakes and Ladders' etc.

Singing games for tiny tots, there was 'A ring a ring of roses, A pocket full of posies, Isha Asha, we all fall down', and the tots pretended to go down.

Like many other things, the origin of these words go back a long time ago, but this one was rather nasty, for it was about the great plague, when victims sneezed a lot before they fell dead.

Wallflowers growing round the wall, we're all little children, we're all going to die except' - naming the child.

Nuts and May, Farmers in his den, The Mighty Duke of York, who was the son of George 3.

Ball games as well as football, were played. The footballer's goal was often marked by the boys' coats. Stotting the ball to see how long it could be kept up, was competitive, with various methods such as 1.2.3. A - Laire etc. Throwing and catching and throwing to each other.

All these past time games were very good for health reasons, developing muscles and getting the blood flowing.

Other singing games were -

Lucy Locket lost her Pocket
The Jolly Miller
Pop goes the Weasel
Looby Loo
Poor Jenny is a weeping
The big. ship sails through the Illy, Ally, O
The farmers in his den
Oranges and Lemons
London Bridge is Falling Down
Nuts in May
Old Roger.

Tippy Cat was another game made of wood. Apiece of wood 6 inches long, with pointed ends had the middle pared away to resemble a square waist. A red hot needle burnt roman numbers on each side. The players in turn tapped the tippy with a stick and recorded the number that came to the top to see who could score the highest.

NEWSPAPERS

Newspapers played a vital part in the lives of people long ago.

For one halfpenny they were very useful indeed.

After the people who could read had finished with them, they could serve as makeshift tablecloths or be used to wrap up the men's baits. When the fire was low a sheet would be placed in front as a blazer to encourage the fire to burn.

Crumpled paper was used to light the fire.

Drawers were lined with paper, and pantry and cupboard shelves were spread with paper, the overhang being cut to make a pattern.

One vital use was for squares to be cut and a pile of them to be threaded with a piece of string to hang on a nail at the back of the netty door. Toilet rolls were unknown here in those days. This was one of the jobs children were able to do as well as collecting piles of unused papers to take to the fish shop and the sweet shops.

Fish and chips were wrapped in newspaper and squares were rolled into cones to hold sweets when sold. The children were rewarded with a few sweets or chips in return for the paper piles.

Of course, there were no nude pictures in the papers, not even of ladies in low cut dresses, and certainly no foul words.

Newspapers were aids to beauty, for strips of them were used to roll hair into curlers.

THE RAILWAY STATION

1837

The Great North of England, Clarence and Hartlepool junction railway formed and constructed an eight and a half mile line from Wingate to one and a half miles north of Ferryhill for mineral traffic instead of going via Middlesbrough Port.

Ferryhill was an extremely busy Railway Station then.

1846

In October passenger services opened between Hartlepool and Trimdon, and later a mineral line to the old colliery. So now Trimdon Colliery was also called Trimdon Station.

Actually the original station was at Trimdon Grange, probably just a stopping place behind the "Swinging Sign" pub in Rose Street (Chapel Row), which of course then changed it's name to the "Station Hotel", but was commonly called "The Duck" after the original landlord.

1851

The Station was built and in the first year it took over £224 in fares. From Trimdon to Wingate was 3d. return.

On Saturdays folk went to Hartlepool for the excursion of one shilling return, they would do all of their shopping and all purchases were then wrapped in brown paper and firmly tied with string. Shop assistants had to be very proficient in these matters. The big treat then was to go to the theatre, there was The Grand and The Empire.

The Empire was a lovely building in Lynn Street and after purchasing entry tickets, you walked up the stairs and through the foyer where there were always comfortable settees around a coal fire. Seated in the audience, it was a thrill to see the fire screen come over the stage, then watch the orchestra come in and tune up. In the interval ,part of the roof lifted for fresh air. Many of the old well known stars made their debut here and its such a pity this lovely old building was destroyed.

Trimdon Station.

Trimdon Station had good staff. The building itself had the Station Masters house, the Ticket Office and a waiting room where in winter a coal fire was kept burning. There was also another small waiting room at the end. The office had a glass covered porch joining with the waiting room where plants hung as well as flowering plants set by the platform. The entrance to the Station was a downward path from the bridge near the store (this bridge was destroyed and the bank lowered in the 1980's). Another entrance from the Trimdon Grange side, via the black path, (which was the only way to travel from the Colliery to the Grange) led through a heavy gate and over the rails. By this gate was a squat brick building where the Hartlepool fish women kept their fish and old prams. There was a signal box and a short row of houses facing the down platform for the railway workers.

09.06.1952

The Station was closed to passengers

01.01.1962

Station closed altogether

There was an early mail train and a quarter to nine train to Hartlepool which carried Secondary School pupils to Henry Smith's School and St. Joseph's Convent. They returned on the four thirty from West Hartlepool.

Many village folk set their chores to the times of the trains, starting washing by the nine o'clock and the ironing by the twelve o'clock etc. The trains passed under the three bridges, the first by the Trimdon Grange Doctors, the next one carried the road from St. Paul's Post Office by the store and the third one was opposite the pit.

Sadly the second bridge was the scene of a tragedy. A "Henry Smith" school boy was leaning out of the window of the homecoming train and caught his head on the bridge. He died instantly.

All of the bridges have now been demolished and the Steep bank lowered. The bank was really steep and it had been a source of entertainment when the Brewery horse wagon had to struggle to get the barrels up to the top to deliver the beer to the pubs.

Under the bridge by the store was the road to the Foundry. It actually was to be the link from the old pit and was to join up to the Station line. However it was found the pit engines (The Coffee Pot one) was too tall to go under the archway so the line was removed and joined directly with the Station. This was the line that crossed the road between Rodwell Street and Luke Street.

Quite a few scholars lived in Fishburn and had to walk from there to get the school train and walk home again at night. The train ran from Ferryhill via Coxhoe, Trimdon, Wingate, Castle Eden, Hesleden, Hart to West Hartlepool. To go to Sunderland, you alighted at Castle Eden to await the connection to the Wellfield Line. The Castle Eden Station always grew lots of lovely flowers.

Traditions

Tid, Mid, Misera, Carling, Palm and Paste Egg Day.

The above names were often recited as the Sundays leading up to Easter Day.

Carling Sunday

Carling Sunday was a tradition of the North East but seems to be now dying out. Carling Sunday was the fifth Sunday in Lent. Carlings are small brown peas and it is thought the tradition may have started when a ship carrying a cargo of peas was wrecked on the North East Coast.

There are various ways of cooking and eating them. Soaked overnight, they can be boiled alongside a ham or bacon shank and served at a meal hot or cold, with vinegar pepper and salt. Some are steeped, dried then fried in butter.

Sometimes they are soaked in beer and served with mint sauce. Children often carried a newspaper packet full, so they could eat them like sweets whilst playing in the streets. Most pubs would have a big dish on the counters full of carlings, free for their customers.

A skipping rope rhyme was,

Tid, Mid, Misera, Carling Palm and Paste Egg Day,
We shall have a weeks play,
Bonny frocks on Easter Day.

Easter

Easter, apart from its religious significances, seems like starting afresh. The winter behind us and Spring with its new life of flowers etc. seems like a new beginning. Even the hens start to clock, and hatch chickens to begin a new generation and it is eggs that play a large part in Easter celebrations.

Nowadays there are chocolate and other sorts of eggs to take the place of the natural ones. Again it was the mothers who did the work. Even if a person did not have their own hens, eggs were quite cheap. It was who could have the bonniest eggs.

In those days, coloured cloth was not always dye proof, some eggs were then wrapped in the coloured materials and boiled, the dyes then transferred to the shells and making a jazzy picture. Onion peelings over the eggs made a nice shade, more so if the names were written on the eggs first with candle grease, so the name remained visible. Whinny (Gorse) flowers were another source of colouring as was tea or coffee.

The eggs were all hard boiled and distributed to all the children. The boys had a grand game called jarping, similar to 'conkers'.

In those days hens were not always confined to a garden shed, but were free to wander the streets, which of course had no made up roads. Consequently they picked up much grit and so their egg shells were really hard.

Two opponents faced each other, holding their eggs ready to jarp, break the other's shell. The winner claiming the losers egg.

This was the time when new clothes were worn if there was any money to buy them, but even so old clothes could be altered and made to look different. If the weather was fine, which it often was there were picnics or visits to the seaside.

Anniversaries

Most children attended a church or chapel Sunday school. They were encouraged to attend by being rewarded with a summer time trip to the seaside. This was usually by train to Hart before charabancs became popular. The Sunday school superintendents took the large washday pans, carrying them onto the beach. Helpers collected beach wood, sticks and coal and with water collected from the farm tea was boiled and served. This day maybe along with Whit and Carling Monday would be the only holiday many of them would get, so it was looked forward to very much.

Another exciting time was the Anniversary. There was much preparation for this. The children would each be given an appropriate poem to learn, then in May or June, for two Sunday mornings they would meet in the street instead of chapel, and sing hymns accompanied by the organist playing the mobile organ. In the afternoon regulars' parents and friends attended the chapel to hear the little ones say their 'piece'. Some little tots were shy and burst into tears but to some it gave them confidence to confront folk and speak well.

The children wore white dresses.

Christmas

Christmas was eagerly looked forward to.

Preparation even began in the late summer. Everyone had their own Christmas cake recipe and it was now they started to collect the contents to make the cake. Nowadays everything is bought ready made in cartons, even to all the ingredients being in one package. In those days shop assistants had to be experts in weighing and packing all groceries. Everything came loose in barrels, crates, tubs or chests. Goods were weighed on gleaming brass scales and transferred into dark paper packets with the tops neatly folded in securely, - no sellotape then. Butter from the tub was patted into ½lb., 1lb. and 2lb. blocks. Tea arrived loose in big square chests. Grapes were in barrels or wooden crates covered with cork dust, which was also used for stuffing toys, oranges were in barrels or wooden crates which children could convert into dolls houses. So everything was made to be useful.

The cake was not made in one day, for there was much preparation beforehand. All of the currents, raisins, and sultanas had to be examined, stalks picked off when seen and then all rubbed in a clean floured tea towel. The lemon peel had to be cut into small pieces and other ingredients prepared.

When the day of the actual baking arrived, all of the cake mixture would be in the large bread bowl and everybody had a stir and a wish. The fire was watched over to get the oven to the exact heat and then a small dollop of the mixture was put on a saucer and baked. This was called the 'trial' and was much enjoyed. Then the whole mixture was put in the tin and cooked.

The same preparation was made for the Christmas Pudding, but they were boiled either in the washpan or in the 'set pot'.

When the cake was cooked, after being tested with a knitting needle it was cooled, wrapped in towels and carefully stored away. Everything came out fresh at the right time, everything being natural and fresh that went into the making, even butter being used as margarine was not yet popular.

We in the North East are lucky between North and South, so we can keep the Southern Christmas cake and also the Scottish Hogmanay- New Year, so some folk cut their cake at Christmas while others keep it till New Year. The custom was that whoever visited the house, friend or stranger they were given a piece of cake and a glass of wine, often home made ginger wine.

The hoops from the butter barrels were collected from the shops and one hoop would be placed over the other to make a sphere and would then be tied. Coloured tissue paper was bought in a packet, cut into wide strips which were folded in half longways, then the scissors snipped the fold half way down all along the fold. Each strip was wrapped around the hoops mixing the colours and then glitter ornaments were fastened around. This was called a Mistletoe and hung from the ceiling. The children's stockings were hung by the fireside on Christmas Eve, in readiness for Santa Claus. An apple, orange and nuts would be found in each stocking in the morning and if lucky maybe a small toy.

More preparation in the early days was making a new mat. Many folk liked to have a new mat to put down for Christmas Day. These were made on hessian or even with a hessian sack opened out. These were sacks used to hold potatoes and vegetables. The material was stitched into the wooden frames. A pair of frames could be 3, 4, or up to 9 feet long. The long ones being used for quilting. They were of stout wood with a folded strip of strong material tacked down one side so that the hessian could be sewed onto it. When all was stitched up one frame had the hessian rolled over it, leaving space for working. To stretch this tight some wide laths with many holes was pushed through slots in the big frames and then stabilised with nails through the lathe holes. A pattern was then chalked on the mat. A favourite was the Prince of Wales Feathers. This was a brown cut out, laid on the hessian and chalk marked around it. Another was the plate pattern. When a plate was chalked round it was moved to cover 3/4 of the first one and so on. Each division would be filled with a different colour and outlined in black, as was the wide border of the mat.

There were two types of mats, proddey and hookey. (Some call it proggy). The only tools were a thick piece of steel tapering to a point with a knob at the top for the proggy clips and a similar tool but with a hook at the end like a large crotchet hook for the hookey clips, (these were often made by the pit black-smiths) From the storing of old clothes the clippings were made. Proddy ones were cut into finger wide lengths, which were then cut into pieces the length of a matchbox. Hookey ones were just the long strips rolled into a ball.

Proddey mats were made by making a hole with the prodder and then using it to push one end of the clips into the hole, making another hole close by and inserting the other end into it. One hand was always underneath the mat to direct and pull the clip. The hookey one was worked right side up with the length of the material held underneath and being pulled up in loops by the hooked prodder. The children were also workers for they cut up the clippings.

The long frames took up a great deal of the room, which was usually the kitchen (it being the only room) and each end rested on a table or chair.

Neighbours often came in and helped to prod and when at least the mat was finished there was a pan of toffee made amid much rejoicing.

The mat would be rolled up and maybe deposited under the bed or on top of one for extra warmth before being laid on Christmas Eve. Some of these mats could be two yards by one and would take two people to take it outside to shake it. Another tradition was to paint or freshen up the fire surround.

Christmas was very much looked forward to but was certainly not a commercial event.

Guisers were in evidence also, that is people dressed up to disguise themselves, woman usually in male attire. They visited houses, for doors were never locked, so they could walk in and be offered refreshments, Some folk made more fuss at New Year and would not cut their cake until then. Just before midnight all doors would be locked and everything was quiet until the buzzer blew and the Church Bells rang on the stroke of midnight. The door would only be opened to the expected caller who had to be a dark man , for a 'first foot'. He was supposed to fetch good luck to the home and to prove it he would have a lump of coal in his hand to put onto the fire. The ashes from the coal fire had to be removed before the stroke of midnight and everything tidied up ready to welcome a New Year.

Sometimes high spirited lads would push all the rainbarrels over so the rain-water would run down the street. These pranksters were likened to the present day vandals, but in a much milder form, for they had no intention of harming anyone. Other pranksters would tie some string to a house door sneck (opener) and fasten the other end to the next door before knocking on the doors. Their reward would be witnessing the futile attempts of the householders.

TRIMDON GRANGE CHURCHES

According to Whelan, book of Durham 1894, St. Alban's Church, a good brick building erected in 1886, partly by subscription and partly by the Colliery owners, at a cost of £800 with sittings for 180 persons. The Wesleyan chapel, built in 1861 will seat 250 persons. Primitive Methodist chapel built in 1892, at

Inside Rose Street Methodist Chapel, Trimdon Grange.

a cost of £650 will accommodate about 400. Christian lay church is a brick structure built in 1891 and cost £300. It will seat 250. It was built in the 'Plantation'. The preachers were not ordained ministers. It was destroyed when the 'Plantation' was demolished. St. Alban's church is still as it was, but has an added room and kitchen. The church members gave their time every Wednesday to provide a luncheon club for the elderly of every denomination. The meals are bought from the Meals on Wheels service.

Folk are welcomed with a cup of tea or coffee, the meal is served, followed by another drink and a game of Bingo. A Community bus brings the pensioners and takes them home again.

The Wesleyan chapel, built in 1861, situated between shops in the front street, but was demolished when the whole street property was destroyed. The Primitive chapel 1862 still stands and services its people. It stands at the top of what was once a busy street, Rose Street, but commonly known as Chapel Row.

TRIMDON COLLIERY CHURCHES

These buildings have not been so stable apart from the Church. According to Whelan - The 1884 Church dedicated to St. Paul, situated in Trimdon Colliery, is a plain brick structure with stone facings, in early English Style consisting of nave only. It was built by subscription at a cost of £1,200 two acres of land being given by the Wilkinson family. The interior fillings are of pitch pine, and will

St. Paul's Church and Vicarage, Trimdon Colliery.

seat 200 persons, a burial ground is attached. The living is a vicarage, in the patronage of the Bishop of Durham : gross value £300 : Rev. Oates Sagar M .A. Vicar. This church was built for the ecclesiastical District of Deaf Hill cum Langdale, which was formed chiefly out of Trimdon Parish. The church still stands in the churchyard as originally but the church yard is now full and a new cemetery is used on Thornley Road. Many of the kerbs surrounding the graves have been removed (by permission) to make grass cutting easier. The Church now has a clock tower which was erected in 1950 which is a boon to the villagers.

Wesleyan Methodist Church and Schools, Trimdon Colliery.

According to Whelan in 1894, the Wesleyan chapel was at the top of the Colliery in 1845 but in 1912 a new one was built at the end of Rodwell Street. The site of the old one was used for the Imperial Picture Hall . When the foundation stone of the new chapel building was laid, Deaf Hill school children had a half day holiday to attend. When the Primitives and the Wesleyans merged, the services were held in the Primitive Chapel and the Rodwell St. Building was used as a training school for out - of - work boys, then later it became a Warehouse for the nearby Gatenby shop.

Trimdon Primitive Chapel.

The original Primitive chapel was a small building next to the Post Office in the Square. This was found too small so in 1900 another one was built at the top of Station Bank. There were high steps to the chapel and low ones to the basement. The original chapel became the Mens Reading Room, but is now no more. By 1994 the Chapel needed repairs, and the upkeep being expensive, the congregation set to work very hard to build a new one on the same site, holding their services in the near by St. Paul's church. In the past, some woman worshippers wore a small black bonnet type of hat because they were in the Pentecostal League. Before the middle of the century, a wooden hut was built next to where the Welfare now stands. This was for the salvation Army and their band. Sorry to say, this was disbanded and the hut had many changes - a bingo hall, a grocery shop, called the tin tops, a car service shop, but it is now empty.

TRIMDON VILLAGE CHURCHES

According to Whelan in 1894.

The Parish Church dedicated to St. Mary Magdalene, is a small stone building situated in the centre of the village, and consists of nave, with north aisles and chancel. The chancel arch is Norman, but greatly depressed, owing to the giving way of the side walls. On the south side of the chapel is a small, round leaded window through which it is said the lepers received Holy Communion. The Church was restored in 1884 and the north aisle added at a cost of £700 and will now seat 150 persons. The living is a perpetual curacy, of the certified value of £21 - 5 shillings, gross income £215. The tithes were commuted in 1839. The parish register commences in 1720. Patron Henry John Beckwith Esq.

In 1811 a new graveyard was consecrated by Bishop Barrington as the area round the church was full. In our time the headstones from the church plot have been laid aside and the surrounding wall demolished. Before this uncaring people had thrown their rubbish over the walls.

Front Street, Trimdon.

Opposite the church was a house which later became a farm house. Monks lived here and when the church bell rang for service, they were able to leave their chores and quickly get to communion. The last tenant was farmer George Cartner, and sadly the house was pulled down to make way for the building of Tremeduna Flats.

This church has a small lepers window so victims of this disease could watch the mass without entering the church to contaminate others. Sherburn House hospital was originally built to house lepers.

St. William's Roman Catholic church was opened January 17th 1864 and has been improved. It serves the three Trimdons *(see booklet written by Cannon Fee)*.

One religious building is lacking in its history. This is what is believed to be the monastery of the white Monks of Hurworth. Although it is in great dis-repair it gives the view and feeling of the church. On old maps there is definitely the symbol of a church, and the land round about is named Purgatory Land, where bones have also been found. It is thought that all documents would have been destroyed in the 1536 -7 dissolution of the monasteries. Perhaps they were hidden as were the deeds of another monastery that a monk hid in a pie he made.

The Leper's Window.

Hence the rhyme of Little Jack Horner, for the deeds would certainly be a plum find.

Trimdon Village Church.

FUNERALS

A funeral in the village was a great, though sad event involving many traditions and superstitions. When a person died, even in the middle of the night, someone would have to go to the local coffin maker's home for the stretcher board. Chosen neighbour would then wash, dress and lay out the corpse on the board which lay over chairs. Special linen was always kept for such an event. White sheets covered the board and there was another to cover the body which was clothed in a white night-dress if female or a white shirt if male. Long, white woollen stockings covered the feet. Sometimes, if there was room, a clothes horse - a folding wooden erection for drying clothes - was at the head of the board and was also draped with white cloth.

When the burial arrangements were made, two chosen neighbours acted as bidders. If a man died two men each wore a black sash across one shoulder. For a woman, female bidders wore mauve and for a child a white sash was used. They would knock on everyone's door and say "You are invited to so and so's funeral, lift at 2 and bury at 3". Of course in those days communities were not so large and so everyone tended to know about the forthcoming funeral. Most Trimdon Grange and Trimdon Colliery burials took place in Kelloe churchyard and it meant everyone walking there. The glass hearse would be drawn by one or two horses wearing lovely feathery plumes as their headgear. The procession of walkers would form outside the house, where the coffin would be brought out and placed on chairs whilst hymns would be sung over it.

Tradition demanded the wearing of black and mourning close relatives would wear dark colours for a year afterwards. If this was not practical, a deep band was worn on the sleeve to show reverence. The white paper blinds at the windows of the deceased were kept drawn not just for the burial but for a few days afterwards. Boiled ham would be bought or a friend would cook a shoulder of ham and make pease pudding, for everyone was buried with ham and pease pudding otherwise it would be a disgrace. Returning from the funeral, tea was laid out and the people, especially the men, congregated outside if there was no room indoors until it was time for the second 'sitting down'. There was one old lady who made a point of attending every funeral in the village. She joined the procession and set off with it but as soon as it left the village she hurriedly returned to be sure of a 'first sitting' at the table. Until the time of fastening the coffin, the corpse would be on view to all the visitors. It was almost an insult if someone did not wish to look at the corpse when the veil was lifted from its face. There was an incident in one of the single houses in the Foundry. Having just one room, space was limited, so the corpse was at the foot of the large bed, which was lying sideways to the door. One visitor had her little girl with her who, of course, had to be very quiet. The child could not see any seat for herself and as she was tired, rested against the nearest backrest which was the end of the stretcher board. She must have leaned a bit too heavily because the board acted like a see saw alarming the assembled company as it and the corpse rose into the air. Needless to say, the house was soon empty.

At these sad times, folk relied on the insurance. When a baby was born it was immediately insured for a penny a week policy. This was continued and when the child grew up and was married it was often given the policy to be continued.

Friends and neighbours were all good helpers in these sad times, everybody being willing to assist. If a person had no money then they would be buried by the Parish in a paupers grave. This was a terrible thing for people to contemplate and it was a matter of pride to be able to pay for your own funeral. People tried to save to buy a headstone with a marble surround or a wax flower arrangement under a large glass globe.

ST. MARY MAGDALEN CHURCH IN TRIMDON VILLAGE.

By Bob Dunn

It can be readily assumed that the present location of the Church was also the site of a Saxon Church. The old English word for wood was "treow" and "duna" was another old English word for hill - the two words together making Tremeduna becoming the Trimdon that we now know today.

Another theory is that the name comes from two other Saxon words, one being "trum" meaning a settlement and the other being "dun" meaning a stronghold. Yet another explanation is that they meant water and hill. The water being the rising of the Skerne and the hill being the Watch Bank.

The basic structure of the Church was put in place in 1146. Extensive alterations were started in 1873 making for a seating capacity of 150 as we know it today. As recently as 1851 it had been regarded as very ruinous. In 1146 the church was in the charge of the prior canons of Guisborough who continued to say mass there until the dissolution of the monasteries by Henry VIII. None of the present fabric of the Church predates 1800 though the single bell has a brass plaque to Brian Lancaster, a former curate, and it is dated 1759.

The small round headed window on the south side of the church is sometimes referred to as the Leper's window. It may have been used for the elevation of the host during mass. Thus the lepers, who had to stay outside, would also be taking part in this solemn part of the mass.

A vault had been built and completed in 1828 and in 1989 during the relaying of the chancel, this vault was discovered. It was entered and discovered to contain four coffins of three adults and one child. They were of the Beckworth family.

The parsonage was built in 1758. It is now referred to as the old parsonage, a new vicarage having been built.

An old tithe map of 1857 shows a national school at the eastern end of the church. It was shown as a small square building on the 1857 map but did not appear at all on a map of 1897.

A hospital for lepers was built by Bishop Pudsey c. 1181 - 1184 and was called the "House of Mercy". It later became a general hospital and is now a very good home for the elderly.

SUPERSTITIONS

Some older people were very superstitious, and many pitmen were also. Some sayings were like bits of poetry.

See a pin and pick it up
All the day, you'll have good luck.
See a pin and let it lie,
Before the night, you'll have a cry.

Bad luck follows if you cut your finger nails on a Friday

Two people washing hands together in the same bowl, made a cross in the water to prevent a quarrel

Red and White flowers together in a vase, depicts a death.

If the feet of a corpse are flabby, it means there will be another death in the family.

If a sheet, tablecloth or hanky shows a diamond pattern in the fold, it meant a death, regardless of it being an untidy fold.

If a picture fell from the wall it was a sign of tragedy even if the cord or string was old and badly worn.

Death in the village always seemed to come in three's

Crossed knives on the table depicts a quarrel, as also boots and shoes placed on the table.

A knife dropped accidentally, heralded a male visitor, if a fork, it would mean a woman would visit.

What falls on the floor comes to the door.

Bringing May (Hawthorn) blossom into the house brings bad luck with it, but a few folk considered it safe if it was placed in a green glass vase.

Bread baked on a Good Friday (every housewife baked their own) never went mouldy.

A new baby could not go visiting until the mother had been "churched" neither could the mother go visiting till she had been "churched" (Cleansed).

When a new baby first visited a house, the householder always gave it it's "3 things", silver, usually a three penny piece for wealth, salt and an egg for health and good luck.

When a baby was carried from its christening at church or chapel, there was always a little parcel to be given to the first child that was met. The child had to be the opposite sex of the baby, and the gift was a piece of Christening cake and a silver coin.

Never cast a clout till May is out.

This may perhaps apply to the month of May, as the May Blossom is very rarely out until June.

If a person breaks something, they immediately and purposely break two or more articles, perhaps a match stick or some cracked china. This act then drove away the bad luck.

When a person was given a present of scissors, a knife or any sharp object, they always had to give a coin, maybe a farthing or halfpenny in exchange, otherwise their friendship would be cut.

When your ears get hot, it is a sign someone is talking about you.

If feet itch it means there will be a walk on strange ground.

If a piece of coal ash flew out of the fire, it was examined to see if it resembled a purse, a cradle or a coffin. Whatever it looked like it was an omen of things to come.

After a sudden death, some folk, as a memorial stopped their clock for a year and a day.

If a miner going to work, found that he had to return home for something he would not attempt to work that day. Also, if he met a woman while travelling to work during the night, it would be a bad omen, and he would not work that shift.

The day the pitmen drew the caribs, the wives did all unusual things to ensure their men got a lucky draw day lot in the pit, such as turning the fender upside down.

Woe betide anyone who breaks a mirror, for that would mean seven years bad luck. Some folk thought that it was lucky for the owner if another person broke it.

Bad luck could be the result if an umbrella was opened up in the house.

Drop a glove and pick it up was another sad tale, but if someone else picked it up, they would get a pleasant surprise.

A person spilling salt had to throw a pinch over the left shoulder to keep the devil away.

Bad luck to those who first see the new moon through a window, but if outside it would be good luck to turn your money over.

No-one should poke another person's fire unless they'd known each other for seven years.

A visitor must depart from the same door as the one she entered by, unless she sat on a chair for a few minutes.

Two spoons accidentally placed in a saucer meant the sign of a wedding.

A flake of soot on the fire bars means a visit from a stranger.

A cure for a child's bad cough was to take them a walk to the Hill Howly (now Wingate Road, Council House Estate) or if possible to take them to the seaside so the cough would be taken with the tide when it went back.

To prevent children taking colds in the winter, a piece of camphor was placed in a little flannel bag, and hung around the childs neck, worn night and day.

For gardeners, the time for setting potatoes was Good Friday and not before.

Some folk would not wear a certain colour if that colour had been associated with a tragedy.

Many folk said that a black cat crossing their path brought good luck.

A right hand itching meant money to pay out, left hand meant the opposite.

Sneezing - Once a wish, twice a kiss, three times a letter, four times something better.

Teatime - Milk before sugar , you're sure to loose your lover.

Two teaspoons together in the saucer denotes a wedding.

Pride goes before a fall.

Superstitions all originated from something in the past.

For instance - unlucky to seat 13 people at a dining table, was because 13 was the number of people at the Last Supper.

People

Lines written by the Late Mary Carberry

The Year 2,000

The year 2,000? Can anyone tell what's going to be - not really ! so, with much yest, I'll do my best, then we'll just have to wait and see.

Will St. Mary Magdalene still stand on the hill, and once more people queue, her pews to fill ?
We'll have to wait and see.
Will Easington Division have a labour M.P. or be won over by SDP ?
We'll have to wait and see.
Will summers be all wind and rain ? while winter sunshine does remain ?
We'll have to wait and see.
Will there be workers, will there be work ?
On the land and under the sea ?
We'll have to wait and see.
Will Deaf Hill keep it's identity. Or become part of Peterlee ?
We'll have to wait and see.
Will Trophy Special be still brewed near,
Voted by Whitbread, their very best beer ?
We'll have to wait and see.
Will children be able to automatically spell,
While adding up their sums as well ?
We'll have to wait and see.
Will the Peterlee Times still be delivered free
Full of Local news and glee ?
We'll have to wait and see.
The Community Hospital will we ever see,
And what will Thorpe's future be ?
We'll have to wait and see.
Will we be living, will we be dead ?
That's something that can't be said
We'll have to wait and see.

Mary, my friend wrote these lines in 1987 and already men do not work under the sea at the coastal pits, Thorpe maternity hospital, which later housed old people, is now no more.

She died in 1988.

Opening of Galbraith Terrace. Chimney stack of old pit in the distance.

Deaf Hill and Trimdon Colliery Local Canteen Committee July 16th, 1921.

MR. SAXTON AND HIS HORSE BILLY

by George Dawson.

Mr. Saxton and his horse Billy had the unsavoury job of "cleaning the midden at Trimdon Grange" Billy was a heavy draught horse, well fed, groomed and sleek, with shining harness with all his brasses glistening. He pulled Mr. Saxon and his cart with as much elegance as was possible for a very heavy horse. Mr. Saxon would sit, reins in hand smiling proudly, for all he surveyed. Billy knew that he was loved and showed it, it was a spectacle to see them on their rounds, "Muck Miden" man and his beloved horse.

One of our favourite games as children (we were not allowed to call them kids) was, "Knocky nine doors". Our door was number 9 was even a victim up to number 28. There wasn't a lot of regard to counting numbers correctly, really, any old door would do. The doors were the old type, plank braced, and well over their real use, so that too much knocking could result in a pile of firewood.

The netties were almost past their prime. The wooden seat had a polo style twelve inch hole, and when my bottom, when a child was much less, I used to balance over this hole in fear of a fate worse than death. I never knew how quickly to get it over with.

The doors to the netties were the same as the doors to the houses, plank wood, opened with a sneck. They were too flimsy to keep out the draughts, and if you took a candle with you to the toilet, it was soon blown out. In the home, lighting was provided by paraffin lamps or candles, four a penny. Some of these lamps were really beautiful, and now in much demand as antiques. They had tall glass chimneys. Usually marked "grifon" or "Pfenic made in Germany". Due to their fragile nature, these glasses had a very short life. They often got blackened with smoke from the wick, and so the slightest knock or draught when being washed would crack them. If there was no spare , then candles had to be used.

Due to the absence of electricity, when we got wireless (Marvellous invention) sets were powered by glass accumulators, 6 volts lead acid type and a grid bias high tension battery, 110 volts.

Periodically the accumulator needed re - charging and we took them to Mr. Hill, the watchmaker. The wireless tuning dial did not have wave length numbers as now. Droitwich, Hilverstone, Moscow, Luxembourg, Riga, Berlin, Prague, San Marina, Vatican, Rome, etc.. The world was your oyster, along with Dick Barton, The Lost World, The man in Black, Paul Temple, The Archers, The Ovaltinies. The latter we could only get at odd times, but B.B.C. London Broadcast racing results. Previous to this wonderful entertainment we had a wireless of sorts, a crystal set, called the "Cats Whiskas".

Only one person could hear it at a time, with the aid of earphones. The whisker had to touch certain points and if you were lucky you may hear something from Newcastle. Ingenious folk tried to enable two people to hear at once, by standing over an aluminium basin containing the earphones.

Procession to the dedication of the Church Clock.

Officials outing in front of the Welsh Harp. Trimdon Grange 1923.

TRIMDON MOTOR SERVICES LTD. 1919 - 1961

by R. F. Spresser

T.M.S. who were one of the pioneers of regular and reliable stage carriage services in the south west Durham, were formed by the amalgamation of two former Trimdon operating concerns, J. S. Grundy esquire with Paul and Seymour.

In 1919 Mr. Grundy purchased a second hand Ford model T, 6 seater bus which had been built in 1916. In 1922 this vehicle was exchanged for another Ford T one tonner with a dixie convertible body. This vehicle was used as a lorry on Tuesdays, Thursdays and Fridays to deliver groceries etc., for Messrs. Broughs of Wingate, on Saturdays by the local football team, on Sundays to special church services. And alternate Mondays it went to Castle Eden and Haswell markets for the Trimdons, Wingate and Wheatley Hill folk. Wednesdays it went to Stockton market and nightly it brought Kelloe folk to the Trimdon cinema.

Messrs. Paul and Seymour also started service with a ford t type and operated between Trimdon and Sedgefield on Saturdays and Sundays. They also ran special services to Winterton hospital on visiting days, otherwise it was used for private hire.

In 1924 J. S. Grundy and Messrs. Paul and Seymour each purchased a further vehicle, both fiats, and decided to operate a joint service to Fishburn for the miners. The tickets for this service were hand made from plain white card and stamped: on having made twelve journeys a person was entitled to a free ride, hence the introduction of the twelve journey tickets which later became popular. It was decided to operate a further joint service from Trimdon Grange to West Hartlepool in 1926 and to operate it as Trimdon Motor Services. Further vehicles were purchased and another joint service started between Trimdon Village and Wingate later extended to Houghton le Spring via old Shotton, Shotton Colliery, Haswell and Easington Lane.

A year later, the West Hartlepool - Trimdon service was extended to Durham via Coxhoe.

Both operators ran their own business until 1929 when they amalgamated to form a company known as Trimdon Motor Services Ltd., with the registered office at Trimdon Grange where it stands today (now empty). J. S. Grundy was manager, and a director, along with R. Paul and J. W. Seymour. The livery, adopted was blue and cream.

At the time, a great deal of competition was felt from United Automobile services, and also from small operators who bought buses and operated anywhere. It was a common sight to see a 'pirate' on the company's stand, and run ahead of the scheduled bus to pick up its passengers. This caused the company many headaches.

However in 1930 the road traffic act came into force, each operator ran a regular service was granted by the traffic commissioners, thus the pirates were shut out.

On the 1st May, 1953 another Trimdon firm was taken over, Alton brothers (Trimdon Ltd.) (A bee line subsidiary company).

The T.M.S garage and offices occupy the land where a large wooden hut stood. This was the main venue for entertainment e.g. visiting hypnotist etc. Later it became Duddins coal depot. The Trimdon Grange picture hall also stood there. Now the offices are all closed and we wait to see what happens in the future.

MEMORIES

By the Late Joe Ebblewhite

The square in Trimdon Colliery was a popular meeting place. Once upon a time there was a market held there on a pay Friday night. The highlight was when travelling theatres paid a visit. These were called "Gaffs". They were owned and acted by a whole family. One family was called Holloway, where their little boy Stanley acted the part of Willie Carlyle in East Lynne. His real mother acted the part of his stage mother who brought tears to the eyes of the audience when she cried over her son - "Dead, and never called me mother". Stanley grew up to be quite a famous character. It was thought that he may have been born in Thornley. Other dramas were plays such as "Murder in the Barn".

The horses that brought the players and the equipment were stabled at the nearby Royal Hotel. This pub was built by John Carter, certainly before 1843. It had a brewery and he originally brewed the beer for the other local pubs. The brewery was later converted into two dwellings, now demolished. The Royal was owned by the Carter family for more than 100 years. It was like a home to the miners when the old pit was starting up being known as a good eating place.

When the colliery houses were built, they had no sinks or drains, but a gutter ran outside the door the length of the street to the drainage sink at the end. All slops, dirty and clean water got "hoyed" (thrown) into the gutter, and also the teapots were emptied into it many times a day. To save journeys to the communal tap, everybody kept a barrel under the spout to catch the rain water which was used for washing purposes.

Between the wars the Trimdons had its own Operatic Society. "The Mikado" was performed in the Victory Assembly Rooms, "Iolanthe" in the Picture drome and when the Welfare was built it was the hall for "The Count of Como".

Thompson's Red Stamp Stores Staff.

Deaf Hill Soup Kitchen 1926, in the school yard.

MORE MEMORIES BY ALLEN TEMPLE

Up the 'Colliery' round the corner from 'Johnny the Barbers' and behind Carters' Royal Hotel was an open area called 'The Square'. At intervals during the year the 'shows' used to descend on the square and then for several nights the evenings were 'lit up' by the fairy lights of various shows and round-a-bouts and the blare of those vividly decorated organs echoed over the village.

Many of the young village 'braves' got good hidings from the boxers who ran boxing booths at these shows. For some time after visits of these booths, certain members of the village community sported 'two lovely black eyes'. Their competitive spirits had been raised by the prospect of 2 or 3 pounds rewards if they lasted 3 rounds in the ring against the young boxers attached to the booth - most probably their fighting spirit had been fortified at Carters 'Royal'.

When Trimdon Station was a thriving business each Monday evening a cattle train arrived and usually 2 or 3 trucks were detached before the train moved on to Wingate and other stations.

Butchers from the Trimdon villages met the train and drove their cattle through the village to the slaughter houses, behind their butcher shops. Needless to say the young boys of the village acted as enthusiastic drovers in helping the butchers. Excitement did sometimes occur when one or more of the bullocks behaved in a rather unco-operative way and decided on their own route to diverse parts of the village, scattering and frightening inhabitants in the process with their unpremeditated visits to back streets, meadows, cornfields etc.

Travelling theatre sometimes pitched a tent in the square and acted melodramas - 'Murder in the Barn' etc. These were called '1d. gaffs'. Stanley Holloway played Little Willie in East Lyne with his father's travelling theatre.

Magic lantern shows were given in the Temperance Hall for 2d entry.

Allen Temple married Cicely Brown and they went to live in Lincolnshire. He was brought up in Station Road in his father's shop where his father had his tailoring business. The shop is still there, our only old fashioned corner shop, run by Mr. Wm. Kirkbride.

THE WHARTON FAMILY

by Bob Dunn

The Wharton family came from Gilling West near Richmond. The first Lord of Trimdon Manor was Humphrey Wharton, who in 1546 was given 400 acres of glebe land as a reward for fighting in a battle against the Scots. This also included property on the north side of the village which had originally been given to the priors of Guisborough from the Durham bishop William de Sancta St. Barbara in 1146.

Following the dissolution of the priory, the patronage of the church passed to the Whartons, then to the Roper family and later, in the seventeenth century to the Woodfields and the Beckwiths. The Beckwith family came into close association with the Parish Church.

JOHN EGAN - BORN 1895

by Irene Collings

My earliest recollection of going to St. William's School was in 1900 when I was 5 years old. The Church was used as a school in those days and they divided it up by putting a large purple curtain across the Alter front. Class one was in the old vestry, the main hall of the Church was divided in two by a large curtain and made a further two classes. Then upstairs, in the choir, was the fourth class.

The teachers were :-

Miss O'Connor - Headteacher
Miss O'Keefe
Miss Roache
Miss Howlie
Miss Grimley

In 1904 we moved into our new school. It was marvellous, we separated into our various classes, we each had a desk and chair, and there was lots of daylight. The school had glass everywhere.

I lived in Trimdon Grange and was born in the pit yard, not a hundred yards from the colliery. They called the street Office Row, the houses were made of wood. We had one room downstairs, one room upstairs. They were named 'one up, one down'.

My nursery days were spent in the pit yard. From my pram I was able to touch the wagons going to and fro from the yard to the main line, that shows how close the houses were to the workings.

The railway station was only three or four hundred yards down the road. The railway had a fascination for me. I got to know the times of the trains arriving at the station and there I was, watching the unloading and loading of the goods van.

Stood outside the station was a flat cart and horse. I used to watch it being loaded up and sent off. The mail was different, it had a small pony and trap to take the mail bags to Thornley and other places.

Going back to my school days, I remember the men who had children going to the Catholic School, laid a path of ashes and cinders, got from the hearths of the fireplaces. It went all the way through the foxgloves from the Grange to the school, just so as to keep our feet reasonably dry and clean, away from the wet grass and mud.

Across the railway crossing in the Grange they built a Cinema called the 'Drome' of course it was silent films and a women played a piano.

We paid 2d. to get in and only got that if we behaved ourselves, of course if we did do anything wrong our Mother's were standing at the door with a leather strap in her hand. Discipline was strict but fair.

Another pastime for men and older boys was handball, fierce and competitive, on a weekend with money in their pockets, they played pairs, for 2d a game on side. Football was another great pastime.

When I was 14 years old I went down the pit for the first time. It was a matter of two hundred yards from my front door to the pit shaft. It was a frightening experience.

Coffee Pot School 1884.

CHANGES

by Shirley Simpson

When my family moved to Trimdon Grange in 1968, we were aware of the close community spirit.

The coal mine had closed down and Trimdon Grange had been classed as category D, which meant there would be no more development, just to be left as it is.

Local people felt the village was worth fighting for, and with the aid of grants they renovated their homes with bathrooms, and inside toilets. As the village improved it was taken out of category D. The Councillor Mr. R. Ellis put a lot of support to the village.

The Council invested money into the environment of Trimdon Grange. The large pit heap which overshadowed the village was removed and landscaped now we see Cows, Sheep and Horses grazing there.

The old shops were pulled down, new shops and houses were built, trees and shrubs were planted , and new people moved into the village.

We have never regretted moving to Trimdon Grange.

PERSONALITIES

Mr. Reuben Ellis, Councillor

Thanks to him with his fellow workers we still have a Trimdon Grange. In 1951 it was in the doldrums and classed as category D, but thanks be to this stalwart, he fought and fought and finally the stigma was removed. Since then, many improvements have been made. The pit heap removed, the old plantain demolished to make way for a new modern housing estate etc.

Mrs. Whitehead, the wife of St. Paul's Church Vicar.

Worked hard in the Community. She ran the Mother's Union and the G.F.S. - Girls Friendly Society, she helped the girls to compete in all the G.F.S. county competitions, dancing, craft work, singing, drama etc.

Mr. Dan Fidiam

Another well known business man bringing trade to Trimdon. He started in a small way by taking watches for repair. Next he opened a shop selling gramophones, then to wireless sets, and television sets after the war.

Mr. George Todd

George Todd who had a broken back due to a fall of stone in the pits, enchanted many people with his lovely singing voice.

Mr. Cecil Hodgson

He was the village cobbler, working in a huge hut at the side of the pit heap where now stands Dr. Sre's surgery. He cycled all round, despite the fact he had an artificial leg.

Mrs. Margaret Ann Harrison nee Thubron of Durham

She came as a young girl 17 years old to teach in the little school by Trimdon Grange crossings about 1874. She roused the women's attention because she wore a hat, which was unusual as the headgear then was a shawl or a man's cap. When Deaf Hill school was opened in 1912 she went there as infants headmistress. During the 1st world war her daughter Mrs. Brown was pressed into service there, as was Mrs. Brown's daughter Cicely. Three generations teaching together and Mr. Harrison also head of the boys Foundry school.

Mr. Leather Watson

The nickname 'Leather' because Mr. Watson dealt in leather, boots and shoes. He had a business in Ellis Street, Trimdon Colliery, which is now called Commercial or Front Street. His fame though was mostly for his "Red Bottle". This was a medicine made of secret ingredients which was a rubbing bottle to cure all aches and pains and a few drops could even be taken inwardly.

His nephew, the veteran runner and long jumper, Len Watson, has the formula and swears by it. Len has travelled to many countries and won numerous trophies. He is still running in 1955. He was born in 1914.

Alderman George Robson

He was a fighter for the workers rights. At sixteen he was one of the survivors of the Trimdon Grange explosion on 16.2 1882. He wrote a poem of this harrowing experience, included in this book.

Mr. Botcherly, Headmaster of the Grange School

Started at the ladies choir. They were all dressed alike and give concerts in the Colliery Church institute, in the first world war. Later he organised a very successful Operatic Society. They played to packed audiences.

Miss Alice Robson

A daughter of the above Alderman Robson, born in 1886, was a well known character. She was a member of the Women's Services of the Crown. In 1918 she joined Queen Mary's Women's Auxiliary, being promoted to the rank of Sergeant Major. She worked for many organisations in Australia. Because of her work in many organisations, she was invited to have tea with the Queen Mother. She was nanny to the famous authoress, Mary Stewart, when the Stewarts lived in Trimdon.

Caleb Henderson

Became a well known heart specialist at Freeman's Hospital. His father followed T. L. Scott in the chemist shop.

Mr. Jim Howie

About 1928, eight of the primitive chapel men held a supper and sang several items. From this small beginning a male voice choir was formed under Mr. Howie's direction, with Miss Lizzie Berriman as pianist. It later swelled to have 60 members but alas it is now down to less. Mrs. Polly Grieves followed Miss. Berriman as pianist until her death when nearing ninety.

Mr. Chris Preston

Was taken a prisoner in the 2nd World War and kept up his fellow mans moral by organising concerts. He is the present leader of the well renowned choir.

Mr. Jack Temple

One of the good bass singers, Jack Temple, rejected an offer to join the D'oyley Carte Opera company.

Mr. Thomas Hill

He lit up Trimdon (village) in 1900 with acetylene gas lighting. His brother had a jeweller's shop in Ellis Street, Trimdon Colliery. He was also a watch maker, one of his watches even now is still working.
This is a copy of the letter sent to Mr. Thomas Hill :- (the watchmaker brother also provided gas lighting)

Trimdon Parish Council Offices
Trimdon Hall
Trimdon R.S.O.
21st October 1902

T. W. Wilkinson
Clerk

Dear Sir,

I have much pleasure in stating that the installation of Acetylene Gas, put down by you, for the above Council in the village of Trimdon, has given every satisfaction, also the generator has proved that your make is undoubtedly first class, we have had the installation two seasons, being put down in 1900, and can therefore speak with confidence as to the success of the installations in the Parish of Trimdon, one at Trimdon Grange and one at Trimdon Colliery (put down by another firm) but these do not give anything like the satisfaction that yours have done.

We have a saving of over one third of carbide from the generator supplied by you, besides a much steadier and more brilliant light, and the saving of carbide alone is a consideration. We have now commenced our third season and the installation is working perfectly satisfactory, in fact I have been repeatedly told by commercial gentlemen who are compelled in the performance of their duties to travel late at night, that we have the best village lighting in the county.

I am Sir, yours truly,

T. W. Wilkinson
Clerk to the Trimdon Parish Council.

To Mr. Thomas Hill
Derwent Cottages
Medomsley R.S.O.

Mr. Fred Hope,

Received the award M.B.E. for all his ambulance and first aid work at the pit and in the village.

Mr. Hill the jeweller also provided gas, as well as designing and making watches.

Good Templars, a non alcoholic society

Met in the Temperance Hall and Messrs. Bill Robinson, Charlie Roddy, Dave Bruce, Harry Langlands and Billy Makepeace formed a band. Mr. Beresford a Salvation Army man was conductor until Billy Makepeace was trained to take over. It was named the Temperance Band but later became the Colliery Band.

Stanley Holloway

This famous actor played in his fathers travelling theatre. These were called Id. Gaffs and were housed in tents. At Trimdon Colliery they acted in The Square : I suppose he excelled himself as Little Willie, to his mother's role in East Lynne. Grown up he was noted for his tales of 'Albert and the Lion'. It is said he was actually born in Thornley.

Mr. T. L. Scott

Was a clever chemist renowned far and wide for his skills. Many people preferred him instead of their own doctors.

We heard of the following people but could not find further information

Old Bunting the horse doctor, Jane Peel, unqualified nurse and midwife. Dick Rickaby, a famous poacher who once applied for the public hangman's job – unsuccessfully. He lived in a shed against the wall in the Raff Yard. It was jokingly said that the shed was so small he slept with his feet poked outside.

Mr. Alex Purvis

He was a miner from Station Town, who started selling boots and shoes, moved to Trimdon Grange and after his wife started a millinery business they opened a shop at Trimdon Colliery, and later another one at Blackhall. Customers came from far and wide. Recently it was sold to the firm of Gatenbys. His daughter Miss Florence, brought many women together by founding the local Womens Institute.

Mr. Leslie Merifield

Trained as a blacksmith at South Hetton Colliery, but finished as Band Sergeant Major of the Cold Stream Guards Band, often having to discuss band affairs with the Queen. For his dedication to music he received the M.B.E.

Mr. Frank Pasquill

Lived in St. Aiden's Terrace., although he was born in the village in 1914. He graduated from Durham University with a first class honours degree in Physics. A Doctor of Science and a fellow of the Royal Society attached to the Met. Office, Air Ministry with posts at school of Agriculture, Cambridge University, Atomic Energy Research Establishment, Harwell and the war Dept. Chemical Defence.

Mr. Colin Jones

Was born in St. Aiden's Terrace, is a doctor of Science and was eligible to be one of the first Astronauts.

Messrs. Joseph Clarke and John Beattie

Received the George Medal for their bravery in trying to rescue a pal from the collapsed pit heap.

Another member of a well known family Abel Lonie.

Joined the metropolitan police force. He became one of the private detectives to accompany the Queen Mother when she reigned alongside her husband King George V.

Mr. Tom Patterson

Son of the "Scatter" Patterson was also awarded the M.B.E. for services in education. His daughter Sylvia was married to Brigadier Commander King at Catterick Camp. When the queen visited there for the 50th celebrations of the Royal Signals, Sylvia, as first lady of the camp, entertained her Royal Highness.

Nurse Welsh

Was Dr. Russells and his son Dr. Toms helper. It was not known if she had received any real training, but she herself would set broken limbs, attend to births and be an all round helper in the surgery. There was no plaster of Paris to help broken bones, just bed and wooded splints and bandages. Babies were vaccinated by taking lymph from one to another. Mrs. Welsh's niece, old Mrs. Herbert was born in one of the original five houses 100 years ago.

Mr. Mick Terrans

Was awarded the O.B.E. and also was made an honorary Alderman of the County Council for his forty years of service. He did a sponsored parachute jump at the age of 80.

Dr. Hugh Russell and his son Tom.

Were the local doctors for many years. Visits were made either by pony and Trap or on foot. They lived in Willowfield House which is still a doctors home. The area round it was believed to be a coaching station when horses were changed over for the long journeys. Castle Eden was another coaching area. The old Doctor and son together give over 70 years of service.

Miss Florrie Purcell

Conducted her father's business and did much helpful work in Trimdon. She was a pioneer in starting the Trimdon Station Women's Institute.

Bobby Cowell

A local lad, Bobby Cowell, born in Salters Lane, Trimdon Grange in 1923. Bobby played for Newcastle United and won three FA Cup Medals with United in 1951, 52 and 55 seasons. Sadly Bobby died in January 1996, aged 73 years of age.

Mr. Owen Willowby

The North American Robbie Football Tournament.

This tournament was established a good many years ago, being open to any country in the world, but all games are to be played in Toronto, Canada.

There are five groups, covering ages from eight to eighteen. Mr. Willowby had been resident for fourteen years in Toronto and was a coach manager to Toronto Ukranians 7,6 F.C.

Returning to England, he organised a first English team to compete in the tournament in 1979, 1980 and in 1981 when they won against the Edinburgh team.

At the age of 76 years he is still working for football as he is the N.E. scout for Tottenham Hotspurs.

Alf Gray

Alf Gray put our village on the map when he formed a dance band. It became very well known and was in demand in many halls round about.

The Times 1854 July 27 p9c

Everyday Life

DAY BY DAY

Monday

This day was often called the Devil's birthday. This meant that it was washing day. Underwear was changed on a Sunday morning and water having been collected, the dirtier clothes were put into water to steep. If the rainwater tubs were empty and dry then all the water had to be carried from the street's communal tap. To carry two pailfuls together without spilling a girth was used. This was a square frame constructed of four pieces of wood or a circle of wood the sides of which rested on the edge of the pails. When the carrier stepped into the frame it was easier to carry the pail in one hand. Some people were lucky enough to have a set pot in a shed or in the lean to back place. This was like a huge iron cauldron set into bricks with iron bars underneath for a fire to be lit. If there was no set pot a huge pan of water had to be kept boiling on the kitchen fire. The white clothes were the first to be put into the poss tub. This was a beer barrel type container with metal bands around it. These could be renewed or repaired by a visiting tinker – often a gypsy. Some washwell powder which was bought in cotton bags was sprinkled in with soap shavings and the possing began - thump thump ! The posser was a thick strong piece of wood which was much thicker at the base. At the top was a piece of extra wood for gripping and holding the stick. If two people possed together it was called double possing, one lifting a stick as the other pounded hers down, thus making quite a rhythm.

The way to the station before 1912.

The whites were then lifted and put through the mangle taking care not to let any buttons go through. Then the dirtiest parts had to be soaped and scrubbed on the wooden table. The soap was a long bar of Sunlight or Lifebuoy measuring about a foot but cut into two pieces. Next the coloured clothes and the towels and , lastly the very dirty pit clothes were done in the same way before the tub was emptied. Everything was repeated three times. The only difference was that the whites had to be boiled, probably with some soda in the water. When the whites were ready for the last rinse it was a blue one. This was managed by squeezing a little bag of Dolly Blue into the water to make the whites whiter. The pinnies, shirt collars etc. Had to be dipped into Robin Starch to stiffen them. Lines for drying clothes were strung across the back street and sometimes just after the line had been filled with drying clothes, the coal cart would come to deliver someone's coal. Then there was a rush to take the clothes off again. The cart just had to lower the back piece, raise it up on end and all the coal would tumble out onto the street to await someone to take their shovel to put it through the small trap door higher up the coal house wall. It was certainly a tantalising time.

What were called lace curtains were very coarse ones and often cream. If these needed washing it was extra work. They had to be well creamed with a cream dolly, similar to the blue one, and then starched. When they were dry two people had to pull at each end to stretch and get them into shape.

When the washing was almost dry, every garment had to be properly folded and placed in a pile ready for ironing. If the day was wet everything had to be dried indoors by hanging them on the clothes horse. This was two wooden frames with bars across and then hinged together.

During all this washing the usual housework had to continue, such as emptying ashes, making dinners and preparing baths for the men coming in from their various shifts plus the cleaning of the pit clothes. It certainly was not an enjoyable Birthday.

Weekdays

The day after washing day was another very busy one. People very rarely had time to iron on washing day. The usual household chores still had to be done as well as the extra ones. There were two types of iron - flat irons and box irons. Both types had to be heated on the fire, even on very hot days. Most fireplaces had a type of bracket hanging on to the bars so that flat irons could be stood facing the bars in order to be heated. If they were put on the fire to be heated, a slipper was used to prevent the clothes from being dirtied. This was a shiny piece of metal which clipped onto the base of the iron before you started pressing. The box iron was a rather heavy affair which had a lid. A shaped stone was put into the middle of the fire and when it was really hot it was plucked out with the aid of a long poker and placed inside the box and fastened down to make it ready for pressing. Manipulating the iron and the fire could be exhausting and dangerous. If some clothes had become too dry they had to be sprinkled with water. When the iron was lifted from the fire it had to be tested in case it was too hot. The best way to do this was by spitting on it and observing the result.

All the ironed clothes were hung on the clothes horse, and sometimes on a line that was stretched across the kitchen so that they were well aired before they were put away. All this work took place in the kitchen and the living room.

An Ordinary Weekday

Often a wife or mother would get out of bed during the night to attend to sons or husbands going to or coming from the pit. There was his bait to be put up - bread sandwiches mostly and a bottle of cold tea or, if he was coming in there would be a meal ready for him. Often the only time a woman had a rest was when she was 'confined' and she had to stay in bed with the baby for ten days or a fortnight and be visited by the midwife. At least she was supposed to stay in bed for this time. This was a chance for neighbours and friends to show their friendship.

Of course the fires never went out completely but were backed up during the night by throwing an extra bucket of coal on. Our fireplace had a very long shelf at the back and we could throw five buckets of coal onto it ready to be raked down onto the fire with the long coal rake.

The ashes had to be raked out from under the bars and transferred into a bucket to be thrown into the midden. Some folk had a square metal box under the bars which made the job a little easier. These boxes and other articles were often made by mechanics at the pit.

Then the mat would have to be taken outside and given a good shake, the floor swept and the hearth washed. If the street had a pavement running alongside the door the part in the front of the door was washed into a half moon shape.

As well as this, the beds were to be made, and callers such as the milk man, yeast man and the grocer had to be attended to. Every day was a baking day if required but some days were social baking days. The big bread bowl was brought out flour weighed and emptied into it and yeast prepared and added. When it was ready it had to be left to rise then mixed by hand into a dough. This was then punched and pummelled, cut up, rolled and put into loaf tins, then laid on the fender to rise before being put into the oven. It was amazing how the women knew exactly when the oven was at the right temperature by feeling the oven knob. There were no thermometers or guides. For stotty cakes some fat was added to the dough and a flattened circle made before cooking. These stotties cold often be seen standing by the window sill to cool and were really delicious when spread with butter and treacle. Tea cakes with plenty of currants were another delicacy.

Friday

Friday was another extra busy day. The main work was concentrated on the fireplace. Most of the fenders were of steel as well as other bits such as the Tidy Betty, the hob over the fireplace and the oven handle. Sometimes these things were trimmed with brass knobs and sometimes there was a strip of brass under the mantle shelf which often sported brass ornaments such as boots, candlesticks and miniature fenders. These were polished shinning bright then the fender was laid aside.

When the ashes were taken out and everything swept the whole fireplace was blackleaded with a substance which came in a tin or a similar liquid which came in a tin bottle. It was applied with a brush and then another brush was used to brighten and polish it. If the oven needed it, it was whitewashed out. Under the bars was also whitewashed a well as the hearth if there was no fancy tin plate for foundation.

The Miners' Hall, Trimdon Grange.

The ordinary chores still had to be done, like cleaning the pit clothes. This was done by shaking the coats and the trousers and "dadding" them up against the wall to remove the coal dust. The pit boots looked more like iron, the leather being so hard and thick. The soles were studded with so many studs that an old knife was kept to scrape out all the dirt.

A pay Friday which was from the time of fortnightly pay was a bit different for some agencies still collected fortnightly on that day. The good housewife would have all the books laid out on the table - insurance books, Purvis, Doggarts,

Fidiams etc. Often the money was on top of each one so the collector could just walk in, collect the money and sign the book if the householder was busy or out the back swilling the yard - no locked doors in those days. Kiddies were sent to the Temperance Hall to pay the Rechabite money (a few coppers) and to the miners' hall to pay the union dues. If the men of the house were at work, someone would have to go to the colliery office to collect their pay on a Friday morning.

Evenings

In the evening, when the lamps were lit, mothers would be darning socks and mending clothes. It was surprising how many holes could appear in socks and stockings especially when the children fell down. Women who liked knitting would be making new stockings and socks and those who preferred to crochet would be making borders for covers using fine crochet cotton. Tatting macramé work and hairpin work was done by a few people.

The children would knit their garters. They would cast 10 or 12 stitches on fine needles and doing plain knitting they would do a long strip which, when finished, was used to tie round their stocking tops to keep them up. This was the reason why plain knitting is called garter stitch.

Another craft was cork or French knitting. This was by means of an empty wooden cotton reel which had four tacks or small nails hammered into the top. Wool was wrapped round them and with the aid of a hairpin , the wool was lifted over the nails. This process produced a strong cord which dropped through the hole in the reel. The cord could then be used for all sorts of things and if stitched into rounds could be used to make small table mats.

Making proggy and hooky mats as well as quilts were other hobbies, the children cutting the clippings and threading the needles.

Boys loved to do a bit of fret work or nailing bits of wood to try to make things.

Games such as Snakes and Ladders, Snap and Ludo were popular. Some folk would not have playing cards in their homes because of the association with gambling and these cards became known as devil cards. Later, however, whist drives became popular. The children amused themselves when they got their "Comic Cuts" and "Rainbow" with Jacko, Tiger Tim etc. On a Friday they had their own newspaper "The Children's Newspaper" edited by Arthur Mee, which was both entertaining and instructive.

Friday night was the usual time for hair washing and bathing the children. This was in the tin bath in front of the fire. Hair was washed in the soft rain water with soft soap and Corax. If curls were needed, then strands of the girls' hair would be rolled up in rags or newspaper and kept there till morning.

Saturday

This was something different. It was a day when there was not so much work to be done in the home. The Saturday trains ran excursion rides to West Hartlepool for 1 shilling return and so many folk took this opportunity to enjoy themselves and shop. Before they went, the older women made sure they took a dish of hot water and washed their feet - just in case they had an accident. Down Lynn Street they would go, up Musgrave Street, across Stockton Street and back into Church Street. "Blacketts" and "Gray and Peverill", "Robinsons" and the "Co-op" were the main stores. The Co-op opened about 1912 and was used to billet soldiers during the first world war.

There was The Penny Bazaar where nothing cost more than a penny and what a lot of things there were! The Woolworth store, painted brightly red, was a little more expensive everything being either 3d or 6d. There was Birk's china shop and SSEades music and piano shop. Plenty of boots and shoes were available at Freeman, Hardy and Willis as well as Public Benefit. Baldesera had the ice cream shop and Fox's sold lovely pork pies. There were some lovely grocery shops and when the goods were bought they were beautifully wrapped in brown paper and tied up with string.

Old friends could be met and gossiped with on the journey round the streets and of course, a visit to the market was always included. The 'shows' were situated behind Lynn Street, the kiddies enjoying the roundabouts and the shuggy boats. The Grand and The Empire were theatres of variety and plays and The Picture House, the largest of many cinemas charged 6d in the afternoons and also held tea dances upstairs. The Co-op had a lovely cafe on the top floor and Birk's cafe by the station was where a lovely cup of coffee could be had along with a tiny jug of cream whilst a small orchestras was playing. This outing was a lovely time for husbands and wives and younger children. If anyone wanted to cross to Old Hartlepool they could get the autocar from the station or go down to the docks and go by rowing boat for 1d or 2d.

Sunday

At last comes a day of rest. Sunday was like a holiday - the literal meaning of a holy day. All week, Sunday was looked forward to being an entirely different day in character to all the rest. No work was to be done at all except, of course, by the poor housewife who had an extra special dinner to cook - beef, pork, Yorkshire Pudding, garden vegetables, followed by rice pudding. Sunday best was also worn. These clothes were reserved for Sundays and special days until such times as new ones were to be had when the originals were relegated to second. The children would attend Sunday School in their Sunday best and then come home to their special dinner after putting on their pinafores to keep their Sunday Best clothes clean. After washing up – in a bowl on the kitchen table – they were often taken for a walk through the fields by their parents. This way the children of the time learned all the names of the wild flowers such as dandelion, daisy, honeysuckle, rose, orchid, scabious, dog daisy, cowslip, dothery grass etc. If they were not taken for a walk in the afternoon, they would often go after tea in the summertime.

No sewing or knitting was allowed – in fact, my grandmother did not allow scissors to be used on Sundays. Only religious books or songs could be used on the Sabbath and no games were played. After Church and chapel evening services, the teenagers would go round the 'hen run'. Older people popped in to visit their friends and if that friend or relative had an organ or a piano there was often an evening of singing - suitable Sunday music, of course! It's amazing considering how badly off people were, there was always a meal set for visitors. For supper there was always a 'fry up' of the remnants of the Sunday dinner. To some, these Sundays might seem rather dull but it was a day that was looked forward to all week. It was a real rest and a change and seemed to be a recharge of battery power for the week of work ahead.

A Sabbath well spent, brings a wealth of content,
And strength for the toils of the morrow,
But a Sabbath profound
What'er may be gained,
Is a certain forerunner of sorrow.

Dancing.

Life was sometimes enlivened by a night of dancing. In the village of Trimdon the only place for dancing was the Parochial School. The partition between the two classrooms downstairs was pushed back and the desks lined up round the room. The dancers could sit on top of the desks between dances. Music was provided by the piano, fiddle or concertina. This once or twice a year event was eagerly looked forward to and attended by folk from the surrounding area.

In Trimdon Grange, dancing could take place in what was once the school, by the signal box at the railway crossings. When the new infant school was built (now the Community Centre) it was taken over as a Church Hall. Another hall in the Grange was the 'Miners Hall' at the top of Tulip's field. Access to the dance floor was by a flight of high stone steps. Tulip's field was so named because the Tulip Family lived in the big square house at the bottom.

Trimdon Station was better off for dancing because it had the Church Institute built in 1912 next to the Foundry Boy's School. The highlight of the year was the G.F.S. (Girls' Friendly Society from the church). This was often by invitation, the cards being written out and delivered by the members. Members also got on their knees and polished the floor and then sprinkled powder all over.

G.F.S. Country Dance Team (Girls Friendly Society).

The pianist could be someone called Newton or Alf Gray, with Sid Thomas on the violin and Sammy Jones on the concertina. This annual dance was held on Shrove Tuesday and each girl always tried to have a new dress for the occasion. The M.C. was often Billy Kennedy who announced each dance and conducted The Lancers.

Another annual event was the Cricket Club dance. This dance would start on Friday night and finish by about 4 a.m. on Saturday morning, thus enabling the men on shift work to get home, washed and changed and still attend the dance.

G.F.S. pageant in the church institute, early 1920's.

The cricketers would be in their white trousers and often they wore white gloves The ticket price was 2/6d and included a sit down knife and fork supper. This was looked after by the wives and mothers of the players. My mother always made and iced a big cake for the raffle. Later, of course, the Welfare Hall was built.

March 17th was St. Patricks day and a grand dance was held as near as possible to that day. It was a very popular occasion.

A very crowded dance was on New Year's Eve in the Welfare when folk from round the county came. The new sprung floor was an attraction as was the dance band led by Alf Gray.

Boys seemed to congregate in one part of the hall, girls in another and very rarely did anyone have the same dancing partner all night. Apart from the waltzes, foxtrots and one steps the dances were ; The Boston Two Step, Valetta Waltz, Erin Waltz, St. Bernard's, Pride of Erin etc. The Barn dance was popular where everyone changed partners. But the really exciting dance was the lancers, a square dance for four couples stepping out by the shouted instructions of the M.C. This was where the men tried to swing the women off their feet.

Other clubs, of course, held dances as well as these annual ones, and Saturday night dances were held in the Welfare - admission 6d (2.5p)

Shops

Trimdon Colliery had quite a variety of shops. Some colliery housewives sold sweets and home made ginger beer from their homes. Next to the Temperance Hall and the Primitive Chapel was Station Town Co-op which could supply all needs from butchering, groceries, drapery, floor coverings etc. Past the station, down the bank, was Paul's, the grocer plus the post office. The telephone number was just simply the number 1. A little further up the street was Sayer's, the printers. The actual printing was done in the shed in the back garden ! Across the road was the bakers and sweet shop owned by the two Miss Robsons. Commercial travellers could stop here for a cup o tea and a snack behind the curtain which divided the shop. At the end of the block was Temple the tailors. The next opening had Swan's sweet shop and further up was Innes the grocer.

Travelling back to the Colliery area, past Alex Purvis, we had Harry Baldwin's the newsagent who later kept a supply of library books for hire for a few coppers a fortnight. Next was a kitchen sweet shop run by Nellie Kell, who also had a tea an sweet shop on Hart Sands. After that was Maughan's the milliners. Next to the opening was Elliot's the drapers run by mother and daughter, Olive, who was a dressmaker. Two butcher shops were next to each other, Jackson and Parkin.

Another well known grocery store was Walter Wilson's. "Leather" Watson's was a boot and shoe shop. Meadow Dairy was a small shop selling dairy goods over

The first shop was T. L. Scott's the Chemist with gas street lighting.

its marble counter. Pringle's was another grocery business attached to a hat shop run by Mrs. Pringle senior. Hill's was a jewellery shop and the father Hill was also a watchmaker and gas installer. Another grocer's shop was Hall's which was at the end of this block which was called Ellis Street. This name and the date of the street's construction was carved on the wall but is now, unfortunately covered over and so its history is now lost. By the pub on the next block there had been a kitchen type pawn shop and at the end was the well known chemist shop owned by T. L. Scott.

In the square was the Colliery post office by the old primitive chapel - later the reading room. This was run by the Stoves family. The post office in Station Road was the main one and the postal address for the Trimdons was Trimdon Station S.O., Co. Durham - S.O. meaning sorting office. Opposite was another grocery business run by another member of the Stoves family. Goods from these businesses could be delivered to the door.

The street names were often very obvious e.g. Pit, Square, Tank (it had a large water tank at the end in case of drought). Bicknell, Lawson, George etc. were named after prominent people and of course, Back, Front, Single Streets spoke for themselves.

Trimdon Grange, like Trimdon Colliery but unlike Trimdon Village, was well supplied with shops in Chapel Row (Rose Street was the post office after it was transferred from Front Street). At the top of Rose Street was Mason's the grocers. Over the crossings into Front Street was a greengrocers owned by my

Commercial Street, Trimdon Colliery.

grandfather, John Edwards. He was the first one to bring bananas into the Trimdons. People thought they were to boil and I heard of one girl who ate one skin and all. Those without gardens could buy a pennyworth of broth which meant a selection of vegetables for broth making. He also had a horse and cart round and was an agent for S. S. Eades of Lynn Street, West Hartlepool selling organs. He was the organist for the old Wesleyan Chapel in Trimdon Colliery.

Quite a big establishment next door belonged to the Tulip family. It was a large grocery shop also dealing in wines and drapery. Part of the drapery was pulled down to make way for the new road which opened c.1920. The Tulips lived in a big, square, grey house at the bottom of Tulip's field. I believe it has since been called Butcher's field but I don't know why.

Past the Wesleyan Chapel there was a variety of shops including Sparks, the undertakers, Barkers, the drapers and a barbers shop. Hilda Roe's was a shop that sold everything including paint and paraffin. There was a branch of the Coxhoe and Cornforth Co-op at the end of this row. Like the Station Town shop at the Colliery it was very large with an upstairs floor and a yard and outbuildings to the rear for the stabling of the carts and horses and the storage of goods. This street no longer exists and the shops have been replaced by trees and grass. The only building left standing in this row is the very first one over the railway crossings from the Dovecote. It used to be The Colliery Inn public house but it has been transformed into a lovely private dwelling.

Front Street, Trimdon Grange – showing the old Dove Cote, the Wesleyan Chapel and part of the signal box. The shop next to the chapel was pulled down to make the new road.

Front Street, Trimdon Grange – from the crossings.

Looking Back

I was born in 1927 at Trimdon Grange at the home of my grandparents. My parents lived in Coffee Pot Street, Trimdon Colliery. It was a street of houses made of old stone. It had one very large bedroom with two rooms downstairs. One was the living room and kitchen , the other was a back kitchen. We had outside toilets and water taps. The toilets were in the back street away from the house. They were in sets of four. Ashes from the fire and kitchen waste was put down the netty as they were called.

In the kitchen we had a very big fireplace with an oven at one side and a boiler at the other. The fire never went out as it heated the water and kept the oven hot. We used the oven for baking bread, tea cakes, pies, cakes etc.. The boiler was always in use for washing clothes, baths, washing up and other household jobs. Coal had to be kept in the back kitchen in two buckets (pails). As they were put on the fire, they were refilled. Coal was free to pit men - they got a load of it every three weeks. Water was also kept in the house in pails, as it was taken out of the boiler. The boiler was refilled as were the pails. I spent a lot of my young days filling coal pails and water pails, but for us it was a way of life so we just got on with it.

We also had oil lamps hanging from the ceiling in the middle of the room downstairs, one on the kitchen table and one in the middle of the bedroom ceiling. If we wanted to go into the pantry or back kitchen we had to use a torch.

Always we had kept a pig in the pantry. Hams hanging up on the wall and legs on the big shelf. Hens were also kept, which meant we always had fresh eggs and bacon/ham. A big allotment was used to grow our own vegetables. Wages were low but we never went short because we were so self sufficient. Proggy and Hooky mats were always in the frames as they were the only things that were hard wearing on the floor.

School Days

We had to walk over half a mile to school, come home for lunch, walk back to school and then come home at 4 p.m. when school finished. After tea we used to change in to old clothes and shoes to play out in. Going for walks over the lodden was something we did often. Also we used to play in the plantation or go to the Rec, and at times we just used to stay in the street and play games.

On Saturdays we went to the pictures and Sundays we went to chapel, then visited grandparents/aunts/uncles/cousins. We also took young children in prams or pushchairs for walks, so their parents could get on with jobs that needed doing. The parents were very grateful, especially on washing and baking days.

When at school we always had to do as we were told, but my school days were happy days. I remember one boy with a stammer. The teacher asked him to read to us. Everybody laughed when he read. Teacher got annoyed and asked him to get her a glass of water While he was gone the teacher told us not to laugh at him again and anyone who did would get the cane. Those nearest to her got slapped with a ruler to let the rest of us know she meant it. No one ever laughed at him again.

Another time I remember was during a cookery lesson, I had been asked to bring in a woolly to wash. some girls had been asked to bring in a collar to starch and others a towel to boil. I put my woolly in the boiler. it came out like a sponge. I took my rice pudding home and after we had eaten it, my brother asked where his pullover (gansy) was. He cried when he saw it and I was told off for not paying attention.

War Time

All my teenage years were war years. The war started when I was 13 years old. We had air raid shelters built at school. I was in charge of the first aid box and my friend was in charge of the drinking water bottle. Cups were kept in the shelters. We all had gas masks and identity cards which we had to carry at all times.

Every window in the village had to have heavy black out curtains or shutters that could be put up at night and taken down at morning. The upstairs windows had black out curtains.

Because we had pigs and hens we did not need to get bacon or eggs. Our ration went on meal and corn for the animals. Again we did not go short of rations as we had friends with a grocery shop. At the end of the month any surplus of sugar, butter, lard, cheese or cigarettes we bought or swapped for ham, bacon and eggs.

Life was hard in the 20's - 30's but because I was a child I never found out. I always had plenty to eat and I was very well cared for by my parents, grandparents and relations. I was taught to knit, darn and sew. We had good neighbours, too, as everyone helped each other.

People from Coffee Pot started to move to Fishburn when new houses were built there. Their homes were not re-let but squatters came to live in them. Squatters were young married couples who couldn't find a place to live. They were very nice people too, young miners and their wives.

Laurel Crescent at Trimdon Colliery was next to be built and that took people out of Pit Street and Tank Street. More squatters moved in.

We were still at war and having to queue for things as they came into the shops. Fruit was scare., especially bananas. We used to queue for an hour or sometimes more and we didn't always get what we wanted. I remember the first peach I ever had. I didn't care for the fur like skin it had but I didn't want to peel it as I thought it would be wasted. Dad took the skin off and I didn't like it at all.

Grandad would pick mushrooms early in the morning and we would have them with our breakfast. He would also pick cress from the beck and we had that in sandwiches.

Life on the whole was very different from today. Pits were the only means of work. Fathers followed by sons - it was a tradition. Shops, of course, had to have workers and there was plenty of competition in that line of business.

In the home, life was different too. When the pit workers came home they were filthy. They had a bath in a tin bath in front of the fire. A clothes horse with an old sheet draped over it made it private. In fact, everyone got bathed like that.
By Iris Johnson

HOUSES

Houses at the beginning of this century were very primitive indeed, mostly made of stone from the nearby quarries. Some of the earliest, I think, were those of Lord Street in Trimdon Foundry. It is presumed they may have been erected for the foundry workers before the foundry was removed to Spennymoor. It is because of these works that that area of Trimdon Colliery became known as The Foundry. Lord Street was a long street with only two gaps, a rough narrow pavement at the front door and a dirt path at the back. The doors were made of tongue and grove panels opening and closing by means of a sneck. There was one room downstairs into which the front door opened, and attached to the back of the house was a lean to over the back door. This was a sort of pantry with a tiny window above some wooden slats which could be moved to let in some fresh air. In the window's ridge were often found eggcups. Folks would recognise the patterns and so remember who lived in the house. Nails on the inside of the back door provided the hanging place for towels or pit clothes. Outside the back door was a large nail on which hung the tin bath which was used by the miner every day when he returned from his shift and by the rest of the family on a Friday Night for their weekly bath. Buckets of water, pails of coal and wash up dishes were kept in these sculleries.

The fireplace was the main part of the living room. It was a huge black leaded affair about six foot square. The fire itself was about a foot and a half up with plenty of space for the ashes to drop underneath. At one side was the boiler which had to be kept full of water so that warm water could always be at hand. The other side of the fire had the oven which often had a round door that let down to act as a shelf when placing or taking out the cooking. There were no thermometers and it was amazing how the housewives knew how to fire the oven to the correct temperature for baking cakes etc. A steel fender would surround the hearth and hold the fire tools which could be up to 28 inches long and which were very heavy. Mainly there was a poker and a coal rake which was used for raking down the coals onto the fire after they had been thrown earlier onto a shelf at the back of the fire. Needless to say, these fires never went out. We had an exceptionally large fireplace which could easily take five buckets of coal onto the back shelf.

All this had to be cleaned regularly every day. The ashes were taken out either by raking them from under the fire and putting them into a bucket or by removing a heavy, and often very, very hot metal box which might have been made by someone at the pit for you and which fitted snuggley into the space under the fire grate. Either way, the ashes were taken and thrown into the midden or the netty. Then the under bars, the oven and the hearth slab had to be whitewashed. Some people had a posh hearth, perhaps purchased by saving their red stamps at Thompson's stores. These comprised a coloured and patterned metal piece which was the same size as the hearth and which only had to be washed. Black leading and polishing also needed to be done on a weekly basis, usually on a Friday.

The sides of the fireplace had flat upright slabs and a mantelshelf resting on top. The slabs were painted various colours at various times and the mantelpiece had a deep frill tacked all round. This frill could be velvet, embroidered linen or crochet work. I remember one crocheted in macramé with covered marbles hanging from it. The mantel shelf would often hold what would now be called priceless ornaments - china dogs, brass candlesticks, brass ornaments, porcelain vases and a tin tea caddy. The vase would often be used to hold any written notes or money to pay bills. Underneath the mantel shelf there would often be a string, a pole or better still a brass rod which was used for drying wet clothes and towels.

On the floor, in front of the fireplace would be a clippy or hookey mat the length of the fireplace. A wooden armchair would stand at one side and a rocking chair at the other. The floor which was made of bricks, stones or cement would be covered with canvas or linoleum.

The window would have a white paper blind. The blind would be tacked onto a wooden roller so that it could be easily renewed when dirty. The so called lace curtains were draped each side and fastened back with crocheted bands. Some folk had what was called a false blind. This was a narrow strip of material with a fancy edge at the top of the window which covered the top of the roller blind.

In front of the window was a square table covered with a baize cloth. This was a sort of oil cloth with a flannelly lining which could be wiped clean with a dishcloth. As well as being used for meals it was used for baking, ironing, washing up etc. Seating was usually a form at the back and the front with a stool or a chair at the end.

A cracket was a useful piece of furniture. As well as being used for a seat it was also used to hold the tin bath for the miner to wash off his grime in front of the fire, his wife washing his back. Some miners in the olden days would not allow their backs to be washed in case it weakened them.

Near the fireplace was often the press. This was a large chest of tall drawers containing the family linen often with a narrow drawer at the top where the insurance policies and the store bills were kept. Some houses had a round table in the centre of the room. These pieces of furniture were of beautiful polished wood. The table would be covered with a plush cloth with heavy tassels. In the centre there was often a family bible on top of which would be a glass dome over a bunch of wax flowers. Round about it would be family photographs in frames. If a large family lived in the house there would also be a bed in the living room where the parents or elderly grandparents would sleep. Elderly grandparents were always looked after by their families.

Access to upstairs was gained by a ladder type staircase. Upstairs was more like a loft with a tiny window. The floor would be covered by cold canvas and as many beds as were needed in the room. If there were more children than there were beds they would be packed in sideways or head to tail. The only way to warm the beds was by wrapping either the heated oven tray or the stone ginger beer bottle, filled with hot water, in a towel. It was a spartan existence. If the family were lucky and had the room, they may have had a dressing table and a wash stand. The dressing table would have a square box for hankies and an oblong one for gloves. The wash stand with a marble top would have a much prized large basin and jug, a soap dish and a tooth brush vase. These, of course, were mostly for pride and show. They would have chamber pots to match.

The rest of the houses were more improved, perhaps by the coal owners. They had an extra sitting room where a prized sideboard would be or a "dess bed". This looked like a sideboard, but instead of drawers or cupboards the front could be pulled down to reveal a fold away bed.

Railway row had a back yard and a front garden. Cuthbertson Street had large back yards and Church Street which looked onto the churchyard boasted the jail house, a room at the end house where wrong doers were locked up until they could be transferred to court.

Though these dwellings were so poor, many were kept like little palaces and much pride was taken by housewives. They must have had to work extremely hard to combat all the dirt and ash dust, having to scrub the floors and wash the outside pavement into a half moon shaped clean area outside the front door.

There had once been some upstairs, downstairs houses running at right angles to Lord Street, one of which was a dame school.

The colliery houses for the old pit were much the same. Pit and Bicknell Streets led down towards the pit and were one up, one down houses. Higher up in the square there were some houses with an extra room downstairs. This room was a sitting room although there must have been precious little free time to actually sit in there.

The first Trimdon Grange Colliery houses were a few very primitive ones next to the pit in the area called "Five Houses Ower the Watter". Next to these was a row of houses with a descriptive name - Duff Heap Row, where Peter Lee was born in number 5. This was next to the first school building next to the signal cabin. Further down the village were the Plantation houses. Originally this land was plantation land, hence the name. The Plantation was made up of the following streets: Walter and Oswald Rows, Cross Row and Thomas Street. Again some were single and some were double houses and you often had to step down into the house from the outside instead of stepping up. The huge and nearby pit heap hovered over these houses. One day during the second world war, the slurry pond on the heap broke and the filth flowed into many of the houses on North Plantation. Later, private building took place on this land after the slums were cleared in the sixties. These were probably the last type of colliery house in Trimdon Grange and the land is now covered with smart modern housing.

The rear of houses in Oswald Row (right) and Thomas Street – The Plantation.

As far as is known the old village of Trimdon (Village) remained largely unchanged although the addition of numerous private and council houses has made Trimdon Village into what it is today.

NETTIES.

A rose by any other name would smell as sweet, but actually Nettie is also a girl's name. Our netties later became known as bogs, closets, W.C.'s (not William the Conquerors) toilets and loos as their architecture progressed.

At one time there were no netties for the poor old Foundry houses. When my grandmother first came to Trimdon Colliery as a bride, she was appalled to find that buckets were used and their contents deposited in the piles of ashes in the back streets. When she said she was returning to her home in Birkenhead, my grandfather built her a contraption at the end of the street in Railway Row.

Some streets later had brick erections built in the back street or at the bottom of the garden. The now extinct village of Hartbushes (South Wingate) had their netties across the other side of the main road to Hartlepool. Good job that transport was by horse power and not petrol driven.

Usually two brick structures were built facing outwards with a yard or two distance between them closed in by a short brick wall. This enclosure was for rubbish. One theory was that they were called netties, because wire netting was put round these enclosures to keep dogs and cats out but no-one I knew ever remembers the netting.

The real toilet place was of brick about a yard wide and about eight feet high. Two or three steps usually led to the wooden door fastened by a sneck latch. Inside there was a short wooden partition reaching from side to side with a lid on the top. In the centre of this lid there was a round hole about twelve inches in diameter and sometimes there was also a smaller hole nearby for children. Outside there was a removable iron plate so that the midden man could gain access with his long handled shovel to clean out the contents : disinfectant powder was then sprinkled all about.

Disasters happened when someone had to rush to the toilet in the dark and did not realise someone had left the lid up, the consequences of which can be left to your imagination. Housewives regularly scrubbed the wooden seat and scoured the floor. Some even whitewashed the inside walls.

The outside steps were convenient for children as they provided handy seats for them to sit on playing with their dollies or make believe shops using boodies and stones for goods and pebbles for money.

Another game for older, resourceful girls was for one of them to get under the lid, after the clearance of course, and put her head through the hole whilst her friend would charge a pin for anyone wishing to come and see a living head without a body.

The so called naughty boys, after clear out day, watched for anyone entering the nettie then they would quietly raise the metal lid at the rear and shove in a bunch of gorse, or nettles. Needless to say, the culprits were nowhere to be seen when the victim got outside.

Old and bedraggled, face wrinkled and worn
An old fashioned lady in clothes ragged and torn
She sits knitting her hands gnarled and disjointed with pain
Her gentle voice singing a sweet lullaby
Grandchildren come to see her
"My sweet darlings" she whispers low
"You play nicely and don't make much noise,
I am tired and weary and my bones need a rest".
Old Molly takes forty winks and dreams of when
She was a young girl, carrying heavy bags of washing to make a living
Her family is poor and she is one of thirteen
No electric washers in her day
She stands at the poss tub saying " I am sick of bloody shirts and dirty
Knickers!"
"My hands are sore and red. I wish Mrs. McGinty didn't have such large
Bloomers, and starching those collars are really hell".
"Soap suds and ironing is all there is to my life?"
"Fiddle the lot of it, I'm sick and tired, Why should I be a skivvy
For somebody else".

Extract from Jean Lister.

TRAVELLING SALESPEOPLE

The delivery in the morning was by the milkman with his horse and cart or horse and trap. He would have an urn of fresh milk from the cow, and going from door to door the housewife would bring out a big jug or a basin. The milkman would then dip his measure can into the urn and pour out the required amount. If the householder needed extra milk later, the children could always take a can for some from the local farm.

Another essential caller was Mr. Holcroft, the yeast man from Wingate. In a large basket he had paper bags of yeast for 1d or 2d. Just calling out yeast, brought someone to the door with their coppers to buy this essential ingredient for bread making.

Another cry was "Any fish today?". This was by a Hartlepool fishwife who trundled an old pram containing fresh fish. A board across the pram was used

The mobile delivery shop, Trimdon Village.

for cutting up the fish. A small sort of brick cupboard was by the station gate to hold her supply of fish so that she could replenish her pram when needed. She brought her fish from the town on the early morning train. The Trimdon people who had fried fish shops had to go to Hartlepool on the morning train to buy and bring their fish home to clean before frying at night.

Periodically, a man would call round selling shoe laces, buttons, ribbons, pins etc. They were carried on a tray held by a leather strap round his neck.

Tramps sometimes visited the streets singing their songs and hoping for a few coppers.

The oilman was another regular. He, with his horse and cart, would sell hardware but mostly paraffin oil. There was no need to knock on each door, just a shout would bring folk out with their cans for open doors looked straight out onto the street. The oil was very much needed to fuel the lamps which provided the light.

Other horse drawn carts came up and down delivering groceries etc. No wonder there were rich garden crops with all the horse manure about.

CLOTHES

Women's Clothes

With the amount of different articles women wore, it must have taken them a long time to dress.

First there was a shift (vest). This was a large, long cambric or linen affair often with short sleeves. Then there was a corset. This was a contraption to help keep a good figure. It was embedded with steel strips and whale bone to keep it rigid, hooked all down the front and with laces running up the back. These laces could be pulled tight to try to make a slim waist. Rich folk could have corsets specially made for them having had their measurements taken and sent off to a specialist firm who would then make a corset to those sizes. These stays (corsets) were called Spirellas.

Trimdon Grange school staff 1913. Headmaster: Mr. Watson.

In the place of the brassieres of today there was a home made affair. It consisted of some material about fifteen inches wide and perhaps over two feet long according to the size of the woman. In the centre was a hole made large enough to fit over the head and there was a tape attached to each corner. The two back tapes were brought to the front and tied and the two front ones were tied at the back. All of these tapes were neatly ironed after washing.

Bloomers or knickers were made of lawn until some thick fleecy ones were brought into production. They were like two legs joined at the top and fastened at the waist by linen buttons or tapes. Next came a flannel waist petticoat. Red flannel was popular as the red was supposed to give warmth. On top of this was another white lawn petticoat with petticoats fastened by tapes or buttons. All these articles apart from corsets would be hand made and very often embroidered in white, using various stitches such as the many sorts of feather stitch. To be extra fancy, especially with the younger folk, a camisole was worn under a blouse. It was similar to a blouse but with short sleeves and much embroidered or trimmed with crocheted lace. Combinations were also often worn; they were like a long vest with two open legs.

After marriage women mostly wore black. Their clothes consisted of a long skirt and a separate bodice (blouse). The skirt would have a short narrow fringe running around the inside of the skirt hem. This was supposed to collect the dirt off the road. The bodice would have a full lining with hooks and eyes fastening down the front, and the blouse itself fastened with buttons. Often they were trimmed with braid or beads and if not made at home they were made by a village dressmaker.

Black wool stockings and laced or buttoned boots were worn, stockings often being home knitted before lisle ones came into fashion.

For special outings, coats and hats were worn. No woman would ever be seen on an outing without her hat. These were magnificent creations and must have been very heavy. They were trimmed with feathers, ribbons, artificial flowers etc. And the hat was secured to the hair by hat pins. Women over 40 or 50 often wore bonnets, smaller editions of hats but kept on the head by wide moire ribbons fastened under the chin.

These hats were rarely bought over the counter but were ordered to be made by a milliner in her shop.

Hair (there was no bobbed hair) was piled upon the head and fastened with numerous hair pins. One fashion was to have two little pads placed either side at the front of the head and another round pad in the centre, then the hair was swept over all. To neaten it up a switch was pinned round the centre pad. A switch was made from hair combings. There was some pride taken in having hair long enough to sit on it. After the hair was combed, the comb was cleaned and the combings collected and put in a china box with a lid that had a hole in the centre. These boxes were part of a dressing table set. When a good amount was collected a specialist made them into a switch.

The working woman was much plainer whilst working. Her hair would be scrapped tightly back into a bun and if she was doing dirty outside work she would often wear a man's old cap back to front. A check apron would be over her pinny and often to keep that clean a piece of old hessian sacking covered that. Women in the home were rarely seen without a pinafore - as though it were a badge of office.

Lucky women would have a fur to wear on excursions often including the animals head and tail. Cheaper neckwear was a feather boa. This was a length of numerous small feathers of various colours long enough to go round the neck and hang down at the sides. Of course, an all black one was kept for funerals.

There were barbers for men but often they just cut each others hair unless there was a special occasion. Hairdressers for women were unknown in the villages until well into the century when permanent curling was invented. This was done by means of an electrical contraption, the victim having tubes strung round her head as if she was strung up. Curling tongs were also heated and used to roll the hair into curls and waves. For naturally curly hair, water waving was used.

Children's Clothing

Girls were dressed similar to their mothers but, of course, they did not have such elaborate hats or such long skirts or dresses. Their hats were mostly straw ones trimmed with flowers or ribbon and with some elastic fastened to the brim at each side and hooked under the chin. Often this elastic got well chewed. Liberty bodices were worn in place of corsets until the child became a teenager.

For playing outside, shawls were worn on the shoulders after folding into a triangle. The ends were crossed over the chest and tied at the back. They were cosy and warm for the chest. The shawls, which were either home knitted or crocheted were very useful. If a woman had to go up the street, she never went without a head covering and so she would often take a shawl, place it over her head and tie it under her chin. Old people often wore them in the house.

Jack & Harry Hoban

In winter, children often wore a little bag fastened round their neck with tape hanging close to their skin. The bag would contain a block of camphor to ward off colds. The tiny ones would have a hanky or a scrap of material which was fastened to their pinny so that they would not lose it. They all wore pinnies for school often nice, white starched ones. All babies, at first, wore very long garments.

All boys were kept dressed as girls until they were five years old and ready to start school. They were then britched. Their long hair was cut short and a penny was given to them. No one really knows why boys were kept in petticoats. Was it because mothers were too busy to see to toilet arrangements or were they afraid that some bad men might steal little boys. For school, boys wore white collars, sort of Peter Pan shaped. These collars would be bought and were made of a celluloid like material so they had to be wiped over with a damp soapy cloth. If they arrived at school with a dirty collar, dirty hands or boots the result was often a cane slapped over their hands. Boys always wore short trousers until well into their teens.

For a very special occasion which called for a starched white shirt, a 'dickie' could be used. This was a stout sheet resembling a shirt front which could be used to cover up the front of a flannel shirt and which was attached to the accompanying collar. The word 'dickie' also meant the extra, outside seat at the back of a small car.

Men's Wear

Men wore vests and linings which were long pants. On the top they usually had a flannel shirt, a waistcoat, jacket and trousers. Trousers were kept up by galluses (braces). Socks were invariably home knitted and boots were laced ones. Caps with peaks worn on a day to day basis for dress, and invariably for funerals, a bowler hat was worn if possible. Bought starched collars were fastened to the shirt neck by studs back and front. Ties could be bought or were

Football winners outside Wingate House.

often knitted by the children. The waistcoat would be enhanced by an Albert and watch. An Albert was the watch chain starting at one side pocket and crossing to hold the watch in the far side pocket. Sometimes instead of a tie, a muffler was wrapped round the neck and the ends tucked into the braces.

To be 'swanky' men could wear spats. These were short cloth gaiters which just fitted round the ankles and a fancy walking stick could enhance the picture further. Long, leather gaiters could be bought for children. A button hook was needed to fasten these to the knee. Heavy boots, long blue stockings and old cast off suits were the dress for pit work with a pair of hoggers, these were like shorts. Men often wore a strip of wide red flannel round their waist. This was supposed to ward off back ache. Sometimes it was a deep circle of knitting called a body belt.

Gloves were always in evidence and women and children rarely felt really dressed without them. Fine kid gloves were often used and before putting them on the fingers, were opened out by means of a glove stretcher. To darn fingers of woollen gloves, a finger darner was used. This was a smooth piece of wood shaped like a finger placed into the glove. A wood darner shaped like a mushroom was used for the frequent darning of socks and stockings.

Pyjamas were rarely seen. The only change in men's fashion was when plus fours appeared but they soon died out as did Oxford Bags. A boater was a straw hat called a straw benger. Trilby hats eventually became more popular than bowlers.

Men mostly smoked a pipe. Rolls of tobacco came with the groceries. The tobacco was cut into pieces and put into the pipe bowl. Ladies twist was like a thick string of 'baccy' and this was taken down the pit to be chewed as no matches were allowed down below. Woodbine cigarettes were 1d. for a packet of ten. A famous song was 'Ten little fags in a fancy packet, Ten little fags that cost one dee'

The main materials used for women's clothes :-

Cotton, serge, nun's veiling, silk, alapeca, satin, tussore silk which had to be ironed when very dry. Cambrie, linen and unbleached calico was also used.

News from the pen of the Late Mr. Arthur Langlands.

December 19th 1848. A most singular accident occurred at Trimdon Colliery a little boy, nephew of a pitman named Dinning, had been sent for some milk. Whilst carrying it home, he fell and spilt it. On informing his uncle of the mishap, the latter threw a bag of gunpowder at the boys head, and the bag, bursting by the violence of the blow, a portion of the contents went into the fire, and the whole exploded.

The boy as well as another child, was killed and the other inmates were badly burned - Fordyce Records.

At this period the village shop sold gunpowder to the miners who had to furnish their own explosives.

Trimdon Colliery and Deaf Hill were renowned for sporting activities, handball, quoits, whippets, potshare bowling, pigeon racing, football and cricket. The ball alley at the Workmans Club was the largest in the county, opened in 1925.

Dempsey Gorton, a famous Trimdon Character, played the first game against Joe Elliott of Trimdon Grange 'Pompey' King of Trimdon Colliery was fives (handball) champion of England in 1884. The first football team in Trimdon was known as Trimdon Heroes.

Markets were held in Trimdon Colliery Square. Lighting was gas on the stalls, a sight once seen, always remembered. Several artists used to attend, they painted pictures and sold them. Men dressed in cowboy clothes using bull whips used to entertain by knocking coins out of the youngsters hands, also cigarettes from mouths of older people. Many families in Trimdon have Welsh names such as Evans, Morgan and Thomas. This is mainly because during the last years of the nineteenth century when miners at Trimdon Grange went on strike, the Colliery owners brought in miners from Wales.

These men brought their families and came here expecting to find work and homes. In many cases, they had to fight their way to the pit through the ranks of the men who were on strike. Soldiers had to be called in to keep order, many of these men stayed, however, and it is their descendants who still have their Welsh names.

REMEDIES

Every Springtime children were dosed with a spoonful of Brimstone and Treacle - for a general clean out, it is said.

A small bag containing a little block of camphor was worn around children's necks all winter. This was to ward off colds which could easily turn to pleurisy which could be fatal. Syrup of Figs was often a Friday night dose.

Three cures for warts :-

1. Dandelion stalk milk squeezed onto the wart
2. Dab the wart with mustard
3. Rub the wart with a piece of beef then bury the meat. As the meat rotted away so would the wart.

A spider's web on a cut was used to stop bleeding.

To cure a sore throat wrap an old sock round the neck.

For a really bad cold a boiled onion placed in a sock and worn on the feet would chase the cold away. Boiled onions at bedtime was also a cure. Making syrup from elderberries with some peppermint was grand for bringing down a fever.

Cumfrey leaves from the hedgerow were very good for wrapping over sprains. Broken limbs were just fastened up with wooden splints as plaster casts had not then been devised. This meant that patients suffering a broken limb were often immobile. Cumfrey leaves were used in easing strains and sprains.

SHOPPING

Mothers usually shopped at the Co-operative stores. At Trimdon Grange there was a branch of the Coxhoe and District Co-op and a branch of the Station Town and District Co-op was at Trimdon Station. This was a good way of saving and these stores provided everything - groceries, meat, drapery, greengrocery and furniture. When a person joined the store he or she was given a personal number which was quoted every time a purchase was made. When the bill was paid the price and number were marked on a small piece of coloured paper. This was duplicated, the shopper keeping one and the store office the other. Every quarter of a year these were reckoned up by the store and by the purchaser and for every pound spent, a dividend was given. This was usually about 10d. or 1/- or 2/- but Sherburn stores sometimes gave as much as 3/-. Unfortunately that was in another village. The shopper could either draw this dividend or let it remain in their store book, thus the store was acting as a bank to their customers. On a Monday, a store girl would visit homes with a book of pages listing all the groceries the customer required. Then she would take payment for the previous week's groceries. The ordered groceries would be delivered by horse and cart on the Friday. The butcher cart and the greengrocer cart also visited the streets so no-one had to carry heavy bags of supplies - everything being delivered to the door quite free. The main orders were for stones of flour and pounds of butter, sugar and tea. These goods would be used for baking and feeding the family for the week.

PIVOTING, JEWELLING, Broken Wheels, PINIONS, REPLACED.

Trimdon Colliery, March 9th 1899

FROM M. HILL,

Clock & Watch Maker, Jeweller & Optician.

Repairs of all kinds executed on the Shortest Notice.

OLD GOLD AND SILVER BOUGHT

Watch & Clock Dials Restored and Repainted.

Watch Cases Repaired and made as new.

Clubs could also be taken out for quilts, Christmas extras, clothing etc. One popular club was the Universal. One person would recruit 20 members who would each pay 1/- a week. This meant that the collector would have a pound in the kitty. Members had been drawn out so that the person who had number 1 could have her goods sent for straight away and so forth. Sometimes a person would come round with Christmas Card samples and weekly payments could be made to have private cards. These were cards with the name and address of the sender printed on them. Children took pennies to clubs at sweet shops for their Christmas goodies. There were other shops, Pringles, Tulips etc. And each shop provided something extra for their customers at Christmas Time, a box of biscuits perhaps.

Thompson's Red Stamp Stores at the top of the Colliery provided a good way of saving. Every customer was given a book of blank pages and for every 4d. that was spent a 4d stamp was given to be stuck in the book. When a quarter of the book was filled it could be exchanged for goods - teasets, towels etc. A full book meant a very good exchange.

When people were without work the only way they could have any financial help was by going to 'Kind Joe' which was a name given to the Parish run by the board of guardians. No one liked to beg from them and if they did get any money from them it was very little indeed.

If a woman was left a widow, the only way she could support her family was by doing washing and working for the better off. The pay for a full day's washing was half a crown. The food was cheap but labour was cheaper. In 1908 pensioners who were 70 and were finished work were given a pension of 5/- and a married couple were given 7s 6d. This happened under the Asquith government.

Sixpence a week was also collected for the doctor so that he could attend the family when needed. A few pennies were also paid into a Rechabite Club to act as a sort of insurance when a person needed help.

Ellis Street – Gas street lighting.

Acknowledgements

It is hoped that this book has brought enlightenment to the young and memories to those not so young.

We, the members of Trimdon Past, Present and History Society, would be pleased to have the loan of any old photographs of the Trimdons, including – groups etc. We have not yet been able to find any of Kelloe Winning or of Trimdon Foundry houses.

Please give your name and address so that they can be returned to you as soon as possible.

P.P. Members to contact are :

Eddie Pike	4 East View, Trimdon Grange	01429 881548
Shirley Simpson	7 South View, Trimdon Grange	01429 880155
Iris Johnson	39 Main Road, Trimdon Village	01429 880827
Eveline Johnson	Dunholme, Trimdon Station	01429 880321
Tony Magee	84 The Meadows, Sedgefield	01740 622167

Our grateful thanks to all contributors for both editorial and pictorial content.

Sedgefield Borough Council's support for this publication was part of its Arts Development Programme.